MURDER AS A CALL TO LOVE

A True Story of Transformation and Forgiveness

JUDITH TOY

MURDER AS A CALL TO LOVE

JUDITH TOY

CLOUD COTTAGE EDITIONS
PO Box 652
Black Mountain, NC 28711
cloudcottage@bellsouth.net
828-669-6000

9 8 7 6 5 4 3 2 1

First edition

Printed in the United States of America
Murder as a Call to Love/Judith Toy
First Paperback Edition
Published by
Cloud Cottage Editions
Black Mountain, North Carolina
November, 2011 cloudcottage@bellsouth.net
828-669-6000
ISBN: 978-0-578-08926-3

Toy, Judith. Includes bibliographical refer-
ences. 1.Forgiveness, 2.Zen and Mindfulness,
3.Murder, Survivor Family Members, 4.Thich Nhat
Hanh: Spiritual Journey, Inspirational, Personal
Transformation.

FAMILY NAMES

Starr Family:

Connie, the mother

Lester, the father

Allen, elder son of Connie and Lester

Bobby, younger son of Connie and Lester

Mark, Connie's brother and Judith's first husband

Lane, Mark's wife

Toy Family:

Judith, the mother

Philip, her second husband

Lily, elder daughter of Mark and Judith

Rachel, younger daughter of Mark and Judith

Ned, Philip's elder son

James, Philip's younger son

Grand Family:

Trina, the mother

Stan, the father

Charles, the son and killer of Connie, Allen and Bobby Starr

Leeanne, Charles's girlfriend

Coyne County Trial:

District Attorney Graham Stone

Judge Jesse Garth

Psychiatrist Raymond Smith

For all beings
May the voice of this book
Be heard in the lands
As a prayer for peace

To protect our family from further publicity, I have changed the names of all people and places surrounding the murders. The facts are unchanged.

–JT

Excerpts from this book have been published in The Mindfulness Bell, Best Buddhist Writing, 2006, published by Shambhala, Right View Magazine, Buddhadharma Magazine, WNC Women, and the Asheville Citizen Times.

The story of the potatoes of forgiveness re-told with permission of the author, *The Tao of Daily Life: The Mysteries of the Orient Revealed, The Joys of Inner Harmony Found, The Path to Enlightenment Illuminated* [Paperback] (2007) by Derek Lin, Penguin Group, www. penguin.com

The Eight Realizations reprinted from *Two Treasures: Buddhist Teachings on Awakening and True Happiness* (2007) by Thich Nhat Hanh with permission of Parallax Press, Berkeley, California, www.parallax.org

The Five Mindfulness Trainings reprinted from *For a Future to Be Possible: Buddhist Ethics for Everyday Life* (2007) by Thich Nhat Hanh with permission of Parallax Press, Berkeley, California, www.parallax.org

CONTENTS

FORGIVENESS IS A FIRE

—a prose poem

Forgiveness is a fire in the belly, like that of the Himalayan monks who can melt snow with nothing but breath, sweat and body heat. This fire begins with the stuff of sorrow, the energy of rage. Suffering. We would ignore sadness and anger at our peril, for they are the kindling of fire.

We place sadness and anger on the hearth of the heart. If we fail to allow the fire to breathe, to feed it its due, it will smolder and burn us alive.

Next, with care, we pause and still ourselves long enough to wake up and see we are burning. An in-breath. We look into the kindling of grief and fury, feel heat on our faces. An out-breath. We see into the eyes of the other—the one we claim is the cause of our misery. Now we are face to face with our nemesis.

We continue to still ourselves, to see deep into the face of our foe. Our eyes lock. Breathing in, we discover not only the cause of our enemy's misdeeds; we find their kindnesses and suffering. Breathing out, we recognize ourselves in the eyes of the other—all our cries of discontent, all our joys, unto generations of our ancestors, all the gardens planted, all the sentient beings killed. Compassion fans the flames, ignites our sorrows.

This is the moment of opportunity. We strike a match to our grief the instant we see our self in the mirror of other—in the other, the mirror of self. Here comes the ball of fire, like the first flame, spit by a spark from Grandfather Fire who made earth and sky from the cradle of cosmos.

Creator/destroyer of universe: our fire sets love in motion, a soaring meteor blazing, transforming. Not to destroy, but to make life. Red, yellow and orange flames rise. Kindness flies out on blue sparks. We fully forgive. We dissolve into love, melt into the light of love. And after the fire, there is rain.

–JT

INTRODUCTION: FORGIVENESS AS GRACE

Everything is burning.

—The Buddha

Forgiving the boy who murdered three of my family was like striking a match to the straw of my grief. I did not set out to forgive him. But it happened—suddenly and without warning. And when forgiveness "happened," it came in the form of what Christians call grace and what Buddhists call *prajnaparamita*, the perfection of wisdom, a kind of liberation.

The boy who murdered my family had stabbed and bludgeoned them to death. Feeling battered myself, six months later I fell into the arms of Zen. I was not looking for a teacher, but a dear friend introduced me to a woman who was a Zen monk. Seeking solace and protection, with her expert guidance I set out on the path of meditation and mindfulness practice, calming my body and mind every day.

Writing for me is meditation. Around the five-year anniversary of the murders, I was sitting in the office at home. Perhaps as a way of sorting out my persistent sorrow, I was writing about the murders. I was deeply afraid of the boy who had hidden in their house until they were asleep and then murdered my sister-in-law and my two teenaged nephews. In my mind, he was a monster.

Suddenly I found myself inside the body and mind of the murderer, nineteen years old, furious, out of control, stabbing and beating. And in that split second I knew he was not a monster, but only a boy gone terribly wrong. In that moment, I completely forgave him.

Like Hui-Neng, (638-713 CE) an illiterate peasant who, grinding rice in the kitchen of a Buddhist temple to the sounds of chanting monks who thus suddenly became enlightened, I felt free. For Hui-Neng, something in the combination of grinding the grain and hearing the chanting of the nearby monks created the conditions for him to become enlightened. He was not seeking enlightenment. For me, forgiveness came through the conduits of daily writing and daily mindfulness practice, grinding and listening. I was not looking to forgive.

Imagining myself in the murderer's prison cell where he was serving three consecutive life sentences, I mentally held him in my arms. I knew he suffered. Indeed, not long after that, he took a laundry bag and hung himself to death in his cell. I will always live with the regret that I did not go to him and say, "I forgive you." But if *he* was not freed through forgiveness, I was.

For the last ten years, I have been writing this book in fits and starts. I have spent hours and days trying to remember exactly how these events unfolded for me, and composing a long section called the twelve steps to forgiveness. I ditched that section. Forgiveness cannot be superimposed from outside ourselves. I cannot tell you anything. There *are* no steps. Forgiveness enters like grace— magic, perfect understanding. As the result of what? Grinding and listening, I suppose–walking through our loss and pain.

———

MURDER AS A CALL

The fire which enlightens is the same fire which consumes.

–Henri Frederic Amiel

"Hello?" The phone call comes in the middle of an ordinary autumn day. *Winter will arrive early this year. Still the gingko tree in our front yard has not yet gone yellow, keeps its fan-shaped green leaves. I am standing at my husband Philip's phone in our office, staring at the charred stone hearth of the unused fieldstone fireplace framed in woodwork painted slate blue. Philip's desk, always dusted, shines in the afternoon light that slants through deep-set windows trimmed in the same blue. His is the tidy desk, mine the stacked and cluttered one across the room.*

It is Mark, Connie's brother, my former husband, who never calls if he can help it. His voice is funny, strangled.

"Jude. I can't...I...I got a call. The police called me at school, asked me to drive down to the station."

"What...what's happened?"

"*Connie and Allen and Bobby are...*" he suddenly lets out his breath, "*dead.*"

"Oh my God, oh my God." *The room whirls, the air smells like a candle has just been snuffed. "No. What? All of them? No! Not the kids! Oh my God. In the car?"*

"*No. They were killed. I don't know. At home. Shot they think. I don't know. They're all gone. Th...all we know,*" as a sob shoots up from his belly and stops at his throat.

"The children too?"

"Yes, both boys...and Connie."

"*No.*" *I am holding my breath, adrenaline floods my system, my knees seem to float in water. I fall into the desk chair, half on, half off the seat.*

"*It's true. I know. Jude. I can't believe it.*"

"*Oh our babies, our babies!*" *and the wheel of my universe turns in such a twisted way.*

Hours later, we learn from Mark that Connie and the boys were bludgeoned and stabbed to death in their beds and Connie raped. The TV and the newspapers are full of the murders, the Starr Family Murders. Mark and his wife Lane, besieged by reporters, seem to be able to handle what is happening. But I know he is not; he has never been good in a crisis.

Now reporters and camera men hang around Mark and Lane's front porch in Parkside, provincial Parkside with its old Coyne County charm, its bridge over the creek, its perfect porches, streets named Hibiscus Lane and Pinetrail Drive. Only doing their job, the media mob pounds on neighbors' doors, slashing the air with their questions.

The murders are reported on the networks that night. Across the county, across the street from Connie, Bobby and Allen Starr's house on Lock Drive in Valleyville, Pennsylvania, Stan Grand becomes the CBS spokesperson for the neighborhood. Grand, a Rambo–like a freedom fighter–loud and exaggeratedly masculine–is the only one who will open his door to reporters: "We'll get whoever did this. We have guns and dogs."

That first night, I awake screaming from a fitful sleep, thinking someone is hitting me hard and repeatedly over the head with a blunt, heavy instrument. I am having a flashback, as if I were the murdered.

If only, mercifully, they had been shot.

A SPARK OF HEAVENLY FIRE
AND NECTAR OF THE GODS

*Someday, after mastering the winds, the waves, the tides
and gravity, we shall harness for God the energies of love,
and then, for a second time in the history of the world, man
will have discovered fire.*

—Teilhard de Chardin

One dark night, alone, the story I dreamed up contained my own death. Suddenly I understood the notion of eternity after death, which I pictured as an endless corridor of doors. Clutching the sides of my mattress, I envisioned myself walking the corridor of forever, pulling open door after door only to encounter yet another narrow hallway with yet another closed door at the end.

Church became our family's second home. Cleveland Heights, Ohio, among the hills east of Cleveland which contains Shaker Lake, is the extreme northwestern edge of the Appalachian plateau. Thanks to my devout paternal grandparents, Charles Harrison and Hazel Carroll Rice—Deegee and Gigi to me—who met in the choir, I never missed nor wanted to miss Sunday School. They lived downstairs in our turn-of-the-century brick and board duplex on Colchester Road. It was they who made sure we got to Church of the Savior every Sunday–to a vast French Gothic Revival cathedral built by Cleveland steel and rubber barons, replete with ornamental Moravian tile floors, a seven-sided pulpit and a four-manual organ with over 2500 pipes. My two younger brothers, Dougie and Bobbie, and I wore starched, formal robes and sang in the children's choir. I can still smell the dust of the robe closet in the cool of our church basement. Mother taught Sunday School to the first graders. On special occasions, I got to sit beside Deegee for one of Dr. Brown's sermons. Light from the sanctuary's huge ornate hanging lamps reflected off Dr. Brown's shiny bald head. From his bird's perch behind the finely carved wooden lectern, he never failed to tell at least one joke per sermon. Always when he told the joke, his voice would crack. So for me, laughter was always part of worship. And song.

There was the feel of Deegee's flowered silk dress, the look of her veiled hat riding on billows of rolled-up silver hair, the faint smell of rose water mixed with candle wax. The unsettling boom of the giant pipe organ, with Mrs. Carl on the keyboard bringing "Holy, Holy, Holy" to an enthusiastic congregation at the top of its form, never failing to give me chills. "Lord God Almighty...Early in the morning our songs will rise to Thee...."

On my first visit to the beauty salon and under the hair dryer, assuming that no one could hear *me* because I could not hear *them*, I sang "Jesus Loves Me" at the top of my lungs to a nonplussed, largely Jewish matron audience. "Little ones to Him belong; they are weak but He is strong...."

The elder, mustachioed Mrs. Carl arrived punctually at our house on Tuesdays at four, to teach me simplified piano arrangements of Schubert, Bach and Mozart on my grandmother's spinet in her living room that smelled of dusty roses and mothballs. My grandmother took me, at age nine, after much home coaching, to an audition for one of the first, if not *the* first, children's theaters in the country. I got the part. We toured the elementary schools with *Pinocchio;* I played Columbine the puppet dancer in a pink tutu and toe shoes. Onstage at my own Roxboro elementary school, my strapless tutu fell down. On another occasion, no one could find the donkey mask, and the donkey was absent, so I had to go onstage with my hair thrown over my face, braying loudly in a mask less donkey suit. I went on local radio shows. I was deeply involved in Girl Scouts. Bemused by my hyperactivity, my fourth-grade teacher–who wore sunglasses in the classroom so we could not detect whom she was eyeing–awarded me straight A's with a caveat: "Judy has too many irons in the fire."

Deegee spent much of her life at home teaching me to project my voice, to sing, to play piano, to walk with a book on my head, to use good manners, to write. She sent me on three-minute forays into the backyard, precisely timed, whereupon I was to return to her dining room and write about what I heard, felt, saw and smelled. On Sunday drives, she urged me to pay heed to whatever we passed—("Judy, use your eyes and ears. Do you see that oak over there? That beautiful Georgian architecture on that house on the left? The Dalmatian that looks exactly like the woman walking it?")

To counter my fear of Dying Forever by age eleven, I enjoyed an active prayer life under the aegis of our upper-middle-class suburban church, undergirded as it was by Norman Vincent Peale's *The Power of Positive Thinking*. I was invited by my parents and grandparents to write the table graces for all our family holiday feasts. I often imagined myself sitting in the lap of the white-robed Jesus pictured in my Sunday School room.

Mother was the calm, consistent safety net of our lives—cleaning the kitchen, packing our peanut butter sandwiches, blowing with amazing force into a police whistle (we never knew how she came by it) always three times, to call me and my brothers indoors. At four feet, ten inches, wearing a size three-and-a-half shoe, she was small but mighty. In the top drawer of the dining room credenza, she kept three ping pong paddles labeled with our names. And she was not shy about using them, although she rarely had to. Mother dug up the worn sheets for cutting out our Superman Capes which we then decorated with crayons, pulled my blonde hair into a neat ponytail sometimes twice a day, mended our scraped knees, and played wild tickle games with all three of us kids after supper and before Howdy Doody.

Growing up with Daddy was like growing up at the front table of a comedy club. He, too, was small—five foot five with shoes on—with a voice so booming and resonant that he sounded six foot four. "Marge," he would yell at my mother from the bathroom in the mornings, "Get my barbed-wire collar!" "What do you need that for?" I would ask, falling neatly into his vaudevillian trap. "To fend off the women," he'd reply without missing a beat. Or while he shaved at the bathroom sink in his undershirt, he would point out the vaccination scars on his shoulders that he claimed were remnants of wings. "She hangs out in the alley, and oh boy, what she hangs out," he would randomly glib over morning coffee. Or, "Don't run through the screen door, Mother! You'll strain yourself." The repartee was constant, as was Mom's laughter.

When I was still in this father-worship stage, Daddy gave me a sapphire ring which I cherished. One day when I could not find it, I panicked. Alone in my room, sinking to my knees on the pink rug that matched my pink princess bed, I turned to God, my heart pulsing fast:

"Dear Lord, please help me find my ring." And God told me to look under my dresser. There, indeed, among the dust bunnies lay my sapphire ringed in gold. Later, in my precocious and picturesque vocabulary, I recounted this story, along with a list of my favorite personal miracles, to a group of Coptic Christians at downtown Cleveland's Olmsted Hotel. (This was after my stage-mother grandmother had me entertain the audience on piano with Rimsky-Korsakov's "Hymn to the Sun," key of C.) After my talk, at Deegee's further insistence, I exhibited my rather average paintings. Later, the emcee commented, "And a little child shall lead them ... for the earth shall be full of the knowledge of the Lord as the waters cover the sea."

I was the warm-up act for the main event, Hamid Bey. Along with the rest of the audience, Deegee was a student of this exotic Egyptian Coptic Christian, a friend of Paramahansa Yogananada who wore a turban and advised his disciples on topics as diverse as UFOs and nutrition. Someone recorded the event on a reel-to-reel tape deck which later a friend transcribed to cassette. Oh, I was a Godly child, eager to please.

At age fifteen, due to my father's unbridled drinking and the effect it was having on our family, I joined the then-brand-new branch of Alanon called Alateen. That year, Western Reserve University had launched a study on the children of alcoholics, and through Alateen, I was invited to participate. I was administered the Rorschach ink blot test among others, and the university researchers declared me a well-balanced young person. I told the tester I would never pick up a drink.

Two years later, I was off to the races as a garden-variety alcoholic. My first drink was at a Hungarian Restaurant in Cleveland where a group of us girls were invited to dinner by a group of boys on the swim team at Cleveland Heights High. Our high, heady evening included champagne flutes and strolling violinists. Full of bubbly and sexual urges, on the air of that balmy summer night, I became my father's daughter.

The second time I picked up a drink, three beers at a party, I attempted to jump from a second-story window after catching my boyfriend with another girl on his lap. A girlfriend grabbed me from behind, turned me around and slapped me hard across the face.

For the next thirteen years, I drank and drank and drank.

MARRIAGE AND CHAOS

Just as a candle cannot burn without fire, we cannot live without a spiritual life.

—The Buddha

At about age fifteen when Deegee died, I dropped my faith like a rock. As a high school senior, I started drinking heavily, alcoholically. My parents advised me to join a sorority and find a husband, in that order. I married young, a good Republican boy named Mark whom I met through my college sorority, Delta Gamma, where I was literally given lessons in how to keep smiling under any and all circumstances. He was Phi Gam. We joined the Young Republicans and went door to door campaigning for Richard Nixon. Mark came from a family of Christian Scientists, a religion that I would skip around for the next five years while I drank myself stupid. I was twenty-two when our first child, Lily, was born. What a miracl I began soaking up Wordsworth's "Intimations Immortality," and understood in a different way t child is father of the man. I was full of unexpressed longings: poetic, sexual, literary, philosophical–all of these masked and dulled by alcohol.

What I always remember like a snapshot about one particular suicide attempt is the Cheerios on the kitchen floor. I can still smell them, nutlike and pungent. It was 1967. Lily was eighteen months old. We were living in a small house with a red door. The house was set back from the road on a quiet street in a northern Ohio village dripping with Colonial charm, a tourist destination known for its waterfall and popcorn shop.

I often walked Lily the half mile to town in her stroller. Mark was teaching public school for low pay. To help make ends meet, I worked no fewer than *five* part-time jobs, mostly editing and babysitting, and tutoring a blind middle-school girl in French pronunciation. I worked as a "lay reader" for high school English teachers, writing half a page of comments at the end of book reports and essays, and ʳiving each paper a numeral grade. One of Mark's ᵈopted teenage sisters had come to live with us the summer, a complication I had no means to ʾle.

ᵑnie, my new sister-in-law, who would be dead ᵗhan 25 years, was also a teen at the time. ᵐissed her sister Dee while she was living ʰio for the summer. Connie's life script ᵒm beginning to end–born a small per- ᵍht hump on her back, her blood par- ᵗ and eventually gave her up for adop- ʳas just six years old. That was when ʰart of Mark's big stoic farm family in the countryside of Coyne County. There were two blood children and six adopted. The girls learned to make their own clothes. The boys milked the cow and did farm chores every morning before first light.

One of Connie's classmates reminisced: "It's amazing what my mind conjures up of Connie. My memories are limited to seventh grade; we were in the same homeroom. Our homeroom teacher, Mr. Roberts, was also our English teacher and our history teacher, so we had two hours of class together in addition to homeroom. And that was such a traumatic time in our lives, because it was seventh grade.

"So I was with her for the lion's share of the day. Our desks, around twenty to twenty-eight of them, were arranged in a semi-circle in front of the teacher's desk. So the first row might have four desks and the second more as the circle became wider at the back. Connie sat in the front row to the far right as I faced the teacher, and I was in the center of the second row. So as I looked to my right she was always within my sight. And what I remember are not actual events or things that she said, or anything like that. I just remember that she was consistent.

"She had that little sort of misshapen body, but consistently, despite that little body, her face radiated joy. Most of the time she wore a little cardigan sweater with a plaid skirt. She was neat as a pin, and it was almost like a Catholic school uniform. She was... obedient, cooperative, and radiating a warmth that never failed. We called her 'little Nee'; that was her nickname.

"She was someone that most people found intriguing because she could always maintain that sunny disposition. She wasn't goofy or loud. We didn't know she was adopted. Nobody knew anything like that. She didn't let anyone get real close to her. She had an air of independence despite the fact that she was little, but I don't think anyone was ever cruel to her. They probably felt the way I did, that she was a very special person. She always seemed to try hard to put forth her best effort with everything. She had an aura of quiet acceptance."

For me at age twenty-four, taking on responsibility for Connie's adopted teen sister, Dee, added to the challenges of a toddler and five part-time jobs. Pour on a lot of alcohol and this was a recipe for disaster. Dee had just left for Pennsylvania. I had desperately wanted her to stay, as she seemed much happier living with us. But Mark's parents felt she should come home and return to school after the summer.

Badly hung over from the night before, my nerve-endings frayed, I remember moving up the stairs in slow motion while Lily played in the kitchen. I was sure no one would know or care what I was about to do.

Opening the shabby medicine chest above the bathroom sink, I glanced in the mirror at my reflection. Puffy and pale. Mumbling again and again, "No one cares about me. No one cares." I was profoundly depressed, not because no one cared, but because daily I was drinking large quantities of vodka. God was dead to me.

As if they were outside of me, my hands found the bottle of tranquilizers prescribed by my doctor–one of many in a string of psychiatrists. In a stupor,

I threw back my head and let pour all the pretty pastel-colored tablets, washing them down with a large glass of water. Immediately, a primal *will to live* kicked in. What had I just done? My body began to shake, severely. Did I really want to die? Now? As the event unfolded, our nearby neighbor and friend, a philosophy teacher and Episcopal priest, happened by.

It was the stormy era of Civil Rights, the backdrop to my shattered life, my questions. Bill Lyle, philosopher and priest, was a key mentor for me– the person who changed my fuzzy mind about existentialism and other things. Through his moving stories of marching with Dr. Martin Luther King in Birmingham, his thoughtful reading of my poems and his attempts at answering my questions about existentialism ("What is it?") and finally leading me to the wonders of Camus and Piaget and a re-reading of Dostoevsky–Bill eventually convinced my husband and me to drop our conservative Republican politics and join the opposition.

After swallowing the pills, I told Bill what I had just done. Everything blurred. Phone calls were hastily made. I do not know who was summoned to care for Lily. I only remember glancing, as Bill helped me out of the house to his car, at the kitchen floor– Cheerios everywhere. The baby must have reached up to her high chair tray and pulled down the bowl.

Bill drove me to Lakeside, the state mental hospital where my current shrink was affiliated. With little hesitation, they admitted me. We learned the pills I ingested could not have killed me. They *did* put me to sleep for a long, long time though, even after my stomach was pumped, a gruesome ritual. The doctors and nurses persisted in asking too many questions, all of which I answered with one phrase: "I don't know."

On admission I was relieved of all sharp or glass objects. "How ludicrous is this?" I thought. "All I would have to do is break the glass in one of the pictures on the wall, and neatly slit my carotid." Nor was I was permitted my shoes. Nurses issued us paper slippers. Three times a day we shuffled obediently into line for our meds. I chain- smoked mentholated Newports, three packs a day. Bill bought me a carton. The hospital kept us drugged. They were proud of their "no-locked-door-policy." I routinely fell asleep sitting up.

I vaguely remember the first phone call with my husband, unhooking the heavy receiver on the black rotary pay phone bolted to the wall of the ward. My morning misadventure had taken place while he was at work, teaching English to junior high school students. He was so enraged he could barely speak. I imagined the color drained from his lips. He only went off to work that morning, and I had pulled this—this trick–attempting to leave him *and our child* forever. Furious about what he saw as abandonment of my family, he spoke through clenched teeth: "How could you do such a thing?"

I was unable to fathom his reaction. I thought now he would finally hear me, but no. His rage only upset and depressed me even more. I blamed him for what I wrongly perceived as his not caring enough. And he blamed me. This was the bottom for me.

Lily contracted a nasty case of diarrhea during my two weeks in the mental ward. When they came to visit, my parents stared in horror. The whites of my eyes looked like broken Easter eggs. Slumped in a chair, I lit one cigarette off another, slurring my words, mostly answering their questions with shrugged shoulders or, "I don't know." Daddy moaned, "Where did we go wrong?" I had a list, which I declined to share.

During the day, we were not permitted to stay in our rooms. A hippie girl brought her own prayer rug and sat in deranged meditation for hours on end in the center of the lounge. For the first time in my life, I was served grits, which looked like maggots. Annie, a stocky six-foot patient whose delusions included a false pregnancy, routinely patrolled the dining hall with her brown plastic tray begging leftovers. "You understand I am eating for two." She was welcome to my grits.

Some people played cards. I smoked and smoked. Wrote poetic fragments in a journal: "What is the meaning of grits for breakfast in Cleveland?" One of the quiet women whom I judged a debutante by the way she dressed, turned out to be a local prostitute. She was soon afterwards murdered in her apartment. The newspapers said her place was loaded with needles and pot. A gaunt pair of teenaged patients who had fallen in love whispered to me, "We're planning to escape."

We were not allowed outdoors.

There were ink blot tests administered by Lakeside's kindly nurses, and more than once, the Minnesota Multiphasic Psychological Inventory

(MMPI). With drug-impaired eyesight, I squinted, trying to focus on the page, to fill in the tiny boxes: "True or false? My soul sometimes leaves my body ... True or false? I have a habit of counting things that are not important, such as bulbs on electric signs ... True or False? I commonly hear voices without knowing where they are coming from."

While most of the patients were obliged to chase their doctors down the hall to schedule a session, my doctor was remarkably attentive, with punctual daily one-to-one therapy in his windowless office. A sixty-ish Eastern European with distinguished graying hair and a Roman profile, he was the unit director. I assumed he was a Freudian: after all, he was European, and he asked so many sexual questions. He instructed me not to keep my legs crossed, but to relax in an open-kneed posture. Because he wanted to see me at his outpatient office–not because of any swift recovery–my stay in the hospital was cut short. After my release, during our first afternoon outpatient session, he literally chased me around his desk. I thought this only happened in cartoons.

As I could ill afford to walk away from the subsidized medical care and free knockout drugs–which I fortified with alcohol–I asked to switch doctors. I innocently reported to the hospital administration their colleague, the unit director's ridiculous behavior. Nothing happened. It was my word against his. I was the loony bin patient; he was the doc.

Soon Rachel came along, our tiny second miracle. Now I had two daughters who were receiving mixed messages. One day Mommy would be high: "Let's write poems together! Let's illustrate them with collage! And let's dance!" And then Mommy would bellow: "You're lying, you little brat. Get out of my sight."

They never knew what to expect. Their daddy was equally confused, gathering me up after I passed out at parties, always making sure to locate my handbag, asking me, "Do you *really need* another drink.?"

A CANDLE IS LIT

Aware of countless wise beings, I calmly light this candle,
Brightening the face of the earth.
– Candle Lighting Gatha, Thich Nhat Hanh

After my release from the hospital but before my recovery from alcoholism in a self-help program, when our daughter Lily was three, Mark and I moved to Countytown, Pennsylvania. There, we rented a brick duplex across Violet Street from the Fann Museum. Connie's husband, our brother-in-law Lester, who would die young of cancer three years before the family was murdered, sold us our first second car for $15–a black Ford beater which he himself had rebuilt on weekends. It ran well.

The houses on our street dated back a hundred years and stood close together. Up heaved by the roots of ancient elms and buttonwoods, the old sidewalks jutted and splayed. On arriving home to Violet Drive from the grocery one afternoon, I was confronted by the corpse of a young buck hanging from a branch of the oak in our shared back yard, blood staining the lawn red. The buck's rack was magnificent! My heart sank. Our next door neighbor was the hunter; he offered to share the venison. They, too, were a young family with one child, a son.

Growing up I took for granted my father's gun rack that hung in the den: that he would keep the guns clean, that he only occasionally struck out to hunt with my younger brothers–these were givens. Also a given: they never bagged a thing—just enjoyed a day of tramping through the woods. For me the idea of hunting was benign. So the dead buck in the back yard was a shock.

It was during the Vietnam War. I had taken a stand against all weapons. My brothers were fighting the war–one a tunnel rat in the US Infantry, one navigating the deadly waterways of Vietnam with the Navy. I knew my brothers were brave young patriots. But I was in mortal fear of losing them. I was opposed to the war, opposed to the use of guns, period.

Shortly after the back yard deer incident, I found my daughter Lily on our front porch with the four-year-old son of our neighbor, the hunter. Lily wore a smocked pink frock with puffy sleeves and patent leather shoes set off by white anklets; in her hands, she held a gray plastic machine gun. My heart flew into my mouth. She was holding the gun just right.

Then came Connie and Lester's first baby, a girl which she carried full term. The baby lived only twenty-four hours. Congenital heart failure. I asked myself how I would have borne such a blow. I would not have. My response was to make enormous amounts of soup and salad, and to keep my doors open for whoever needed to come and mourn. Connie was slow to recover.

Around 1970, Mark and I began attending a colorful hippie "underground" church, where I would make sure to get the communion goblet passed back to me for seconds. It helped to cure my hangovers from the Saturday night parties with the very folks in the next pew. I remember coming to after a blackout, precariously balancing on some man's shoulders at one of these parties. Everyone was looking up at me.

MYSELF AS MURDERER

*It is best if we do not listen to or look at the person
whom we consider the cause of our anger. Like a fireman,
we have to pour water on the blaze first and not waste
time looking for the one who set the house on fire.*

−Thich Nhat Hanh

It was 1971. My younger daughter, Rachel, was
less than a year old when I discovered I was pregnant
again. I knew when, where and how it had happened.
Choosing to end the pregnancy was an informed
decision: I knew my options. I had already read *Our
Bodies, Ourselves,* by the Boston Women's Health Book
Collective. Under the chapter heading "Feelings
After an Abortion" are pro-choice testimonials:

> *I felt huge relief. I knew from the moment I
> found out I was pregnant that having an
> abortion was the right thing for me. I felt
> the same way after the abortion and ready
> to move on with my life.*

My friends supported me in my decision.
They talked about it with me and came to
the clinic, too. I was a little tired for a day
or so afterward but that's all.

For abortions, you had to go underground in Pennsylvania in 1971. Or you went to New York for a legal procedure. In New York, I took a cab to the respectable, abortion clinic that looked like a good hotel in a good neighborhood on Manhattan's Upper East Side. There I meet unruffled young women who were accustomed to using abortion as a means of birth control. I felt free. It was the newly liberated seventies, and I knew my rights. In other corners of the city, women were burning their bras. "I can damn well decide what to do with my own body," I thought.

What I did not take into account was the fact that it was not just *my* body anymore. A new life was stirring.

The counseling provided by the clinic was done in production-line style and left little room for questions or second guesses. I was assured by the staff that my surgery would be quick and clean.

It made me sick, their vacuum procedure. One moment I was pregnant and the next moment I was not. I had already felt the tentative flutter like butterfly wings in my womb when I allowed the abortionists to suck out the life of my child. This was a grievous insult to my body, mind and spirit, not to mention those of the unborn.

Afterwards, they put us in a row of cots on clean sheets and fed us packaged crackers and little cans of tin-flavored orange juice and V-8 while they monitored our blood pressure. Mine dropped dangerously. They raised my feet, propping them on two pillows. In no time at all, the crisp nurse attendants informed me I was ready to go. I was not ready to go. I had not eaten a meal since midnight the night before, and yes, it is fine, they said, to consume a normal dinner.

In the restaurant before the meal was over, I rushed from the table with the clean white table-cloth and vomited all of it into the public toilet. Home again in Pennsylvania, I was in dire pain with serious cramps, losing blood at an alarming rate.

Three days later, I found myself in the emergency room of the local hospital where I was administered a thorough D&C to correct the sloppy job done by the expensive New York abortionists.

In my family and among my friends we did not talk about it. I drank heavily to drown my unformed, unexpressed guilt and sorrow.

A few years later in therapy I spent long over-due hours sobbing, labeling myself a butcher. My self-contempt knew no bounds. I felt I could never forgive myself. My therapist explained that because our culture still does not accept the choice of abortion, there is no rite for mourning the deaths of our unborn. Thus, young women like me become depressed, drink or use drugs, numbing the grief in whatever ways they can find.

Valentine for My Unborn

It is dawn. She is bent to her loom.
Deliberately, the Navaho mother
makes her mistake in the weaving

a break in the bright continuum
small opening in the top
of an otherwise perfect design
an escape for the spirit
from the maze of her rug
that the couple who buy it
to hang on their foyer wall
will not notice.

I think of you this way.
Having cut short your life too late
I have paid. Oh, child
the world is full of predators
whose victim you will never be:
time, for one, its black and finite cage.
There are others in the sky, on the ground:
angwantibo, galapagos hawk
who feed on soft beetle grubs
and dead sea chicks.

It was dawn when you moved in me
one last time. "Goodbye," I said.
"I'll think of you forever."

I made a pact with a close friend, Ingrid, to phone her when I was coming apart about the abortion. She promised to do the same when the sadness or guilt surrounding her own abortion became too much to bear. Over the years, we have kept our promise. But it would be many years before I could resolve my guilt and forgive myself.

EARLY RECOVERY

*That something was wrong finally got through to me.
"What's the matter?" By then he did not have to tell me.
Just as the birds know where to go when it rains, I knew
when there was trouble in our street. Soft taffeta-like sounds
and muffled scurrying sounds filled me with helpless dread.*

"Whose is it?"

"Miss Maudie's, hon," said Atticus gently.

*At the front door, we saw fire spewing from Miss Maudie's
dining room windows. As if to confirm what we saw, the
town fire siren wailed up the scale to a treble pitch and
remained there, screaming.*

"It's gone, ain't it?" moaned Jem.

"I expect so," said Atticus. "

–Harper Lee, *To Kill A Mockingbird*

In the spring of 1974, I was thirty-one years old. My girls were seven and two. I kept asking myself, "What am I doing here?" Once again, I found myself institutionalized, this time without the balm of pharmaceuticals to mask my feelings. Again, I was thinking of ways to end my life. One day, I paced like a caged cat through the garden of the alcohol rehab, imagining myself hanging from a tree. On another day, I patrolled the parking lot for a set of keys dangling from any ignition, a way to escape. Here, unlike the last loony bin, we were at least allowed outdoors. I walked and walked.

Wearing a fuzzy pink sweater, my hair in pigtails, I would sit cross-legged on the living room floor of the rehab. The air was always thick with cigarette smoke. Following testing and interviews, the rehab counselors proclaimed my emotional age to be thirteen. I vacillated, as thirteen-year-olds do, between behaving as a grownup and reverting to infantile tantrums.

My part-time job was as a notary and legal secretary for the Legal Aid Society in Countytown, working for idealistic young attorneys. I would sit at my electric typewriter with tears washing my face as I transcribed the sad "indignities" in divorce cases for welfare recipients. As I was the only notary on staff, the law office sent a courier with some papers for me to notarize during the month I lived at the rehab.

One morning I breezed in late to my group therapy session. "Sorry, guys. I had business to take care of for my attorneys, papers to notarize." That did it. My counselor took issue with my arrogance *and* my disregard for the importance of therapy, and she put me on the "hot seat" in a classic version of seventies confrontation therapy (get their confidence, then strip them of everything). Enduring the hot seat meant you got screamed at by counselors and others. "Who do you think you are?" growled my counselor. "Somebody special, that you don't have to get your butt to group on time?"

"Oh no, Miss High-And-Mighty doesn't have to join us this morning. She's way too important," suggested an old woman. Others mumbled their agreement. The derision went on for a good twenty minutes, escalating to shouts. This was the hour I was stripped of any remaining shred of dignity. This was gang humiliation. I felt something like a worm—but a worm doesn't know it's a worm. Everyone in the closed little world of my "family" group had turned on me. This was the bottom of the bottom of the barrel. No, I was *underneath* the barrel.

In a pool of tears and mucous, I numbly stumbled off to the lecture hall, our next class. Sobbing as quietly as possible, I heard nothing much the lecturer had to say. In my mind and heart, with an arrow shot by the venom of the group–*my* family group who had just betrayed me–I called out silently to God, "Please take this garbage away, *please!*"

Suddenly, I was charged with light. My body relaxed completely; my aching belly no longer taut and sore. Lightness and beauty poured over me onto my skin, soaking every follicle of my hair, every organ of my body and bones, every cranny of my weary mind and spirit. At that moment there was nothing I did not know or understand. God was as near to me as my own teeth. So this was the God Dr. Brown had preached about, the God of Jesus Loves Me, This I Know. This!

About a year later, Connie called with a strange confession. "I'm sorry I haven't been very friendly lately," she said quietly. I hadn't really noticed, I told her. "Well, when I found out you were an alcoholic, I felt somehow betrayed. It took me a while to figure it out. I had put you on a pedestal."

"And I fell off, huh? Hard?"

"Yes, I guess so. I've always admired you so much, like a big sister."

"Well, maybe we should just be good friends, just sisters," I offered. Connie, as usual, capitulated.

By 1975, I decided to fetch myself up as a free-lance writer. As I was able to stay sober and keep my brain unfazed, I was also able to sell what I wrote. The first article was a humorous piece–everything I had ever done to my hair, including the time it turned green because I used too many "silver drops" to tone down the bleach—for the Sunday magazine of a Philadelphia metropolitan daily. When I saw my byline for the first time, I pinched myself, laughing and dancing around the room.

My work eventually led to a regular column in that magazine, and to other assignments, notably for the Boy Scouts of America, whose home office was in nearby New Jersey. Freelance writing gave me an ideal outlet for my intellectual and literary longings. Whatever interested me, I would research and write about. This included stream-watching, hang gliding, scuba diving, ocean sailing, the joy of sex–the vintage seventies book by that title, which I reviewed under a pseudonym–small craft airplanes, gourmet cooking, wood working, little theater and the fine arts. "Finding out" meant I had to try it all, which meant I learned to hang glide, scuba dive, fly (took one flying lesson) and sail, and gain a smattering of, ahem, countless other skills. In the meantime, regular meetings of my self-help group were my medicine, not only to keep me well, but also to teach me how to live life on life's terms.

I decided to commute by car and train the two and a half hours to New York City to the New School for Social Research. There I took a one-and-a-half-hour weekly poetry class with Carol Muske, then Carol Muske Dukes, professor of English at the University of Southern California who has been a continuous presence on the American poetry scene.

I pinched myself again when I won the Dylan Thomas Poetry Award and stipend at the New School. "Recipient of the Dylan Thomas Poetry Award" was a line on Carol Muske's book jacket! I was learning for the first time to create my life and happily live in it. My spirit was waking up.

Lily tells me when I came home from rehab I was a different kind of mommy. There were many less ups and downs, many less accusations and recriminations having to do with her and her sister. I stopped hitting them both, period. Sober, I was able to pour some of my creative juices into parenting. Still I felt like a teenager at Back To School Nights, where I thought parents were supposed to be mature, officious PTA types. Remembering rehab and my thirteen-year-old diagnosis, I realized I was learning slowly how to be a grownup.

Early in my sobriety, in 1973, I read Hermann Hesse's *Siddhartha* with that amazing enlightenment scene modeled after the Buddha's, and I knew I had encountered the truth. Tentative and shy about the ways of meditation, I began waking myself at 5 or 5:30 before Mark and the girls got out of bed, slipping downstairs without my coffee or cigarettes, and sitting cross-legged on the carpeted floor of our office to meditate. Well, *trying* to meditate. Getting distracted more often than not. Recalling that crazed meditator from the loony bin. Having wildly un-Buddha-like thoughts and sexual urges. Not knowing what to do with my mind. Would I ever be able to put away the sins of my past?

Ninety days clean, I was asked to speak at my local group's meeting. Telling my story, I was still clearly in the "victim" stage—the stage that justified my drinking without restraint. I was still telling my story as if someone had done it *to* me. I heard myself speak of how my father's alcoholism, and my brothers having to fight in Vietnam, and my husband who does not understand me, were all to blame. I was free of the alcohol, thank God, but not free of blaming. And nowhere near ready to forgive others or myself. I heard myself, and I did not like what I heard.

FROM THE FRYING PAN

Love is a fire. But whether it is going to warm your hearth
or burn down your house, you can never tell.

–Joan Crawford

In 1979, five years sober, I left home with only my clothes, a well-used brown Colt station wagon and my poetry books. My first marriage was over—irrevocably ruined by, among other things, my alcoholism–and I was not yet ready to forgive my husband for not understanding me and for countless other trumped up reasons that helped me do what I had to do—leave. I had taken steps toward forgiving myself, but only baby steps. To support myself, I wangled a full-time job at a drug and alcohol counseling center in downtown Countytown as a receptionist and PR person. One of my first tasks after leaving home was to find two cots for my daughters, Lily, now thirteen, and Rachel, eight, which I placed in one corner of the living room of my tiny one-bedroom efficiency, at a place in the countryside called, believe it or not,

Liberation Farm. Will I ever forget the printed sheets and pillow cases I bought for them–scattered with Kliban's cat cartoons–black and white cats wearing fire-engine red sneakers? Suddenly unmarried, alone for the first time in my life, I often felt like a fish out of water or maybe a cat in big red tennis shoes.

Lily was angry. Rachel clung to me. Aunt Connie, Mark's sister, and Uncle Lester helped smooth the transition for Mark and the girls. She invited them over a lot for Connie-cooked, wholesome meals. Because of the marriage breakup, my girls got to know their cousins, Bobby and Allen better than ever. Mark and his sister bonded, too. Mark and I shared custody, although since I was the home-leaver, or home-wrecker, depending on whom you were talking to, I became the neighborhood pariah. The parents of one of Lily's girlfriends refused to allow their daughter to visit my apartment. Mark wanted me back. There were no books on what to do next. I was seen as a lost woman. Funny, though, I felt instead like I had just been found.

Partly I was found by a man named Philip Toy, whom I had met in the same week twice—once in a poetry workshop at the old Swan Hotel in Lambertville, New Jersey, and once at a self-help meeting in Countytown. Shortly after my departure, we started seeing each other, and he fell right away in love, wanting to move in with me then and there. I held him as best I could at arm's length, wildly attracted, warning him that I was fresh out of a fifteen-year marriage, not having even remotely dealt with the confusing issues surrounding that. But despite my staunch resistance, I was falling too.

Philip was the divorced father of two boys–James at six and Ned at eight–a chemist and poet and jazz pianist. It was his intellect that slayed me–that and the fuzzy voice he used when reading poems to me, especially over the phone. He could play the piano like I never could or would. I could only play the notes on the page; he could improvise. He played everything from Scott Joplin to Chick Corea and Bill Evans to Billie Holiday. He introduced me to the lives and lines of Dylan Thomas and Walt Whitman, Gary Snyder and the Beats. I was still reading the old-timers: Neruda, Wordsworth, Sappho and Hopkins. And like many a good ex-drunk, I had read and re-read the suicidal poet-twins, Sexton and Plath. Philip and I had both sung in the church choir as kids, both sung solos at church and in school. Drama was his minor in college. We were both born in 1943, both in recovery, both reading Alan Watts, two kids each. How could a couple of struggling poets have more in common?

Struggle was the operative word. I was skinny, nervous and agitated, ill-equipped for the unmapped universe of divorce and re-coupling. We entered counseling, especially to help with parenting issues on which we never fully agreed. We felt like a litter of pups piled together, all cold noses, paws and tails, fur flying. Our two boys and our two girls were like oil and water. The day Philip and I moved in together, Ned and James tried to lock Rachel in a closet. I was appalled with the boys' table manners, or lack thereof, their musky smells, their muddy shoes, their wildness. I suffered from extreme attacks of guilt and loneliness. My feelings of guilt for ending the marriage and making my children suffer stabbed at my belly. I had a severe bleeding episode that ended in D&C number two in the hospital. I would ask God to remove my guilt again and again. I could not forgive myself, but perhaps God could and would. At dusk on the days when the girls were away with their father, I wandered like a hungry ghost from room to room.

Our squabbles were dramatic and legendary. Once I broke my toe when I kicked Philip's boot. Another time he broke the little finger on his right hand when he punched the papa-bear chair in a choleric fit. Once out of retribution–"I'll show him," I thought–I went to my room and read every single poem in my Anne Sexton collection. On another occasion when spring literally rained on my parade, I kicked a picnic basket down the basement steps. There were pickles all over the ceiling. And yell? They must have heard us in the next county. Once Philip lay down in the driveway so I could not take off in the car without running over him. An artist friend of ours later made this scene into a sunset cartoon gift with the caption: "As the sun slowly slips into the West, the bucolic Toys disagree over who shall fetch the daily mail…"

Somehow, we would tuck these fights away and go make love. Then they would be forgotten, at least for the moment. My theory was it was good for kids to see a fight resolved, if not the combat itself.

The eighties were our Camelot years. Philip kept asking me to marry him and I kept saying "not again." In the mornings, we would read our "little books" of spiritual inspiration together. I got a copy of Ram Dass's *Grist for the Mill,* in which he states the best reason for marriage is when a couple are householders who share a spiritual path. This I saw as a reason to marry Philip, so I said yes. As the den for our four pups, we found a farm to rent, nearly 300 years old, a Colonial fieldstone manor house on 70 acres of corn and wheat fields in a place called Sloeberry, outside of Countytown. The May day we married on the front porch beneath two buttonwood trees so big at the base that five kids holding hands could barely encircle them, Philip and I read poems to one another. He wore a grey morning coat and I a borrowed, finely-seamed, cream colored Mexican wedding dress from a friend's third marriage. Lily choreographed a dance to "The Wedding Song" and spun across the vast lawn in a white wraparound film of a skirt over white leotard, her long hair flowing. I baked our three-tiered wedding cake with a vase for real flowers sunk into the top layer and cooked for 14 people the night before the wedding. I met Philip's father for the first time that evening. Our parents were meeting each other for the first time, too. In the full knowledge that Philip's father was a teetotaler, non-smoking Southern Baptist, my father's first act was to offer him a Camel cigarette.

There were hundreds of daisies, a stone barn flanked by a spreading elm, a potluck picnic "happening." The IRS seized Philip's bank account, and we found we were flat broke on our wedding day. Somehow, we managed the ceremony with alacrity. We were married by our friend Lyn, a newly minted minister specializing in liturgical dance.

We invented our own vows which included poems and hymns but not "until death do us part." We promised each other everything else, and both of us wept for joy.

Each morning after the honeymoon in San Francisco, I would wake up to Philip's freshly brewed coffee, and sit at the dining room table with a cup in one hand and a cigarette in the other, power smoking five cigarettes to jump start my day. There was much to accomplish. In order to stay available to our four children, and perhaps to have more time with one another, Philip quit his job as chemist and we started a public relations business at home. Our total assets were an Olivetti-Underwood all metal manual typewriter and a ream of paper. Our office was in the library, the old section of the house with its random-width pine floorboards, deep-set windowsills and ash strewn fieldstone fireplace with brick hearth. With its two separate doors to the outside, we found this room, once a settler's cabin, ideal for hosting our clients.

Out went the struggling poets and in came the entrepreneurs. For these were our three-piece suit, chamber-of-commerce days of the eighties when everyone seemed to be scrambling after their MBAs, if not acting the part. I arrived in high heels at the chamber, learning to work a room with my business cards. We composed brochures and press releases and planned special events. The children rightfully complained because we often brought our business to the dinner table.

They did not much like the altar I set up in the upstairs hallway, either.

"Mudther," Rachel would wail. "Don't you realize I have to bring my friends through this hallway?" I was still trying to meditate in the mornings. Some mornings. Lily married at twenty, the same age I had married Mark. For weeks in secret, I sewed for them a satin wedding quilt the color of orange creamsicles, put together with squares decorated by family and friends. Each stitch a kiss. The wedding shower at our farmhouse was one of the last times I saw Connie. She wore a pastel-colored cotton dress with a flower in her hair—and she smiled. Connie always smiled.

Connie's quilt square was an embroidered heart on lace over calico, delicate, romantic and old-fashioned, like her own heart. I cherish a photo of her at the wedding shower—smiling in spite of the fact that her husband is dying of a fast-growing cancer—flanked by the other women, our hands like pale flowers circling the quilt we presented to Lily, our tangible symbol of family love.

Lester's cancer had appeared first as a persistent cough. Only months hence, it took his life. While he was dying, our daughter Lily's wedding was a cheerful event in a Presbyterian Church with a reception at an old water mill converted to a restaurant. During the festivities, I found it hard to look at Lester, his skin grey and lusterless. Like his dad, a brilliant engineer and an inventor, Allen loved to tinker. Lester bequeathed Allen his reconditioned 1979 Chevy Lumina which became the boy's most cherished possession. Later, after school, Charles Grand from across the street on Lock Drive in Valleyville, and Allen labored over the Lumina for hours in the

Starr's garage while Charles's parents worked away from home. Connie remained even-tempered and cheerful in spite of her sudden widowhood, in spite of the Herculean task of having to raise two teenage sons on her own.

Mark felt a certain responsibility to his sister. After Lester's passing, Mark and my girls appreciated spending more time than ever with Connie and her two boys. They vacationed together in Mexico. In Cancun, Rachel and her cousin Bobby drew close, sharing teenage secrets, sneaking a beer. Also at this time, Rachel drew closer to Connie and began confiding in her what she could not tell her father or me. I was glad they had each other, because I fully trusted Connie.

Philip and I found literary friends–artists and writers who met with us in coffee houses, workshops and galleries. Our best friend and peace activist, Ingrid, was the daughter of a well-known abstract painter and the mother of a fashion designer, as well as a multi-talented painter in her own right. On weekends, the three of us would hang out on the quaint streets of New Hope, Pennsylvania, on the Delaware River where the New Hope School of painters formed and left its indelible historic mark.

It was Ingrid who first told me of a small peace community, Village des Pruniers, in the Bordeaux region of France, Plum Village. How charming, I thought, a community dedicated to world peace. The moment I heard the name, I felt drawn in some way to go there. Or does time fold in the quirk of an instant and make it possible for one to see the future? Sometimes while sitting in meditation at my home altar, I would imagine Plum Village.

Money was usually scarce. When Philip and I needed to beef up our kitty, we sold a potter friend's seconds or Ingrid's late father's handmade picture frames at the local flea market, or we hosted a Saturday yard sale to raise the rent money. To my exasperation, Philip would pull anything out of the house, even a wedding gift, and sell it for two dollars. Another way we supplemented our income was by taking in boarders, housemates. Most were in recovery and most were in a life transition of some kind. More pups for our den.

Ironically, for a recovery household, we once hosted a champagne art opening with two-hundred guests and a string quartet. We removed the paintings from our walls and hung the show of a fine arts photographer who had taken a year to photograph our farm, and who was our PR client. The next day, the show opened in a local gallery. Philip and I were invited by an arts organization to apply for a Pennsylvania Commonwealth grant to do poetry-in-performance at the dusty little theater situated over a downtown fencing studio and ice cream parlor. We got the grant.

I became temporarily obsessed with the idea of androgyny, and developed a poetry-in-performance piece based on that idea. At the end of my time on the stage, I remember sitting down on the apron, looking intensely into the audience and adding a line from Thich Nhat Hanh to explain the idea of interconnection between male and female: "If you are not there, I am not here."

Taking advantage of the large size of our home, we hosted poetry readings–creating and running the publicity and housing the poets. Guggenheim fellow and Pulitzer Prize winner Stephen Dunn, the New York poet Lloyd Van Brunt, and several lesser known literary lights read to our community. Philip and I started our own version of a poetry slam which was wildly popular with poets, the media and the public. Selecting the winner meant dangling a rubber chicken on a stick over the heads of the contestants while measuring the intensity of the din created by the mostly un-sober audience. We hosted this event weekly for a couple of years until the rants became too drunken. There were plenty of competent hosts waiting in the wings to take over, which they did. A couple of our poems went into a book–*Live at Karla's*–that emerged from the erstwhile slam at Karla's Café on a small-town corner in Pennsylvania.

I was invited as a visiting poet into the schools. That was the start of over a decade of school and museum residencies, work with the young that I adored, that served somehow to soften me. I was accepted to study with Bread & Puppet's Peter Schumann, and began making giant parade-sized puppets. This led to more visiting artist's residencies. Philip and I hosted the New Hope Arts Academy for kids at our farm. And we started a Gifted Young Writer's Summer Academy, with visiting famous writers. I lived for several weeks at an artist's colony in Virginia to finish a poetry manuscript, meeting and falling in love with octogenarian Australian novelist, Joan Colebrook. Before she died, we visited her at her dune house, Truro, Cape Cod, where we met the poets Annie Dillard and Marge Piercy, and where I got myself a job on a whale watch boat. The job interview consisted of one question: "Do you get seasick?"

Taking a job on the high seas was to reward myself for quitting smoking–but not without considerable difficulty–because my dear firstborn Lily was pregnant, and I flatly refused to be a smoking grandmother. First the alcohol. Now the cigarettes. What next? After 13 years of drunkenness, and after 28 years of two packs a day, I was free. And in an odd turn of events, for the first time since my childhood, I felt free to live up to my ideals. If I had known then what grim event would finally oblige me to "walk my talk," I would have turned on my heels and run.

At almost the same time, in May of 1989, three weeks before his slated graduation from high school, Charles Grand enjoyed the academic status of sitting in the top two percent of his senior class. An all-A student, Charles was scouting Drexel University where he planned to major in engineering, in the footsteps of his parents. Three weeks before his slated graduation, he refused to take a detention for skipping class. Charles walked out the door of Ridge High and never returned, never graduated.

He stayed home, refusing to cut his hair or shave. Connie was worried about Charles. Then, unknown to his parents or his grandmother or his neighbors, or the Starr family across the street, Charles began leaving the house to stalk the neighborhood at night.

THAT LAWN-DARK NIGHT: OCTOBER 15, 1990

He burns.

His figure dominates the mountain,

and the giant torch of his body fills the jungle.

–Thich Nhat Hanh, "The Fire That
Consumes My Brother"

Connie always felt a motherly concern for Charles across the street, always a latchkey kid and friend to her boys. While Allen and Charles bent to tinker under the hood of Allen's Lumina, Connie would appear in the doorway of the garage with a smile and a tray of toasted cheese sandwiches and ginger ale.

The night he murdered them, Charles hid in the dark of that same garage, waiting for them to return home from a shore trip, to go to bed and sleep. He knew where the house key was hidden. I try to imagine his state of mind as he crouched in the darkness,

— 49 —

waiting. Was he afraid? As far as anyone knows, Charles was not on drugs. But his body and brain had to have been crazed. A monster waited in the dark.

After he was certain they were asleep, he crept upstairs and murdered them one at a time, in their beds in their separate bedrooms—with a knife and a hammer. He raped Connie. I pray she was already dead.

After committing the crime, he stole the Lumina, using it as his getaway car. With the bloody murder weapons on the back seat, Charles drove nonstop to Florida and reconnoitered with friends. His total cash take, the only motive anyone could ever ascribe to the murders, was upwards of five hundred dollars. He had been so close to the family that he knew certain details: that each year during the triple coincidence of Connie's, Allen's and Bobby's birthdays in early October, Connie would tuck their birthday money into a particular desk drawer in the dining room. Charles had known precisely where to locate the cash. After the killings, he took with him the family TV, some clothing, a cache of Connie's makeup, some jewelry and Bobby's Nintendo set.

If there had been violence and rejection at home, no one at Charles's school knew about it. Or they were not talking. Charles did not fit the killer mold: he came from an upper middle class, respectable family and as far as anyone knew, did not abuse drugs. However, after his strange and sudden exit from high school, Charles had stolen his father's home arsenal and his car. His father pressed charges against him, and while awaiting the disposition of this crime, Charles jumped bail and went to Florida with Leeanne, his girlfriend.

In Ft. Lauderdale after his getaway, Charles told fifteen-year-old Leeanne the story of the murders in gruesome detail: how he had planned the crime, how he had carried it out, the order in which he killed them, how Bobby had cried out to his mother for help, how he was planning to return to kill his parents and grandmother. Leeanne called the police.

Officers drove her to the Ft. Lauderdale station and ran a video camera while she clearly recounted the story Charles had told her. On tape, they captured Leeanne applying Connie's stolen lipstick to her own lips.

Charles was immediately picked up and arrested by Florida police officers and remanded to Countytown, Pennsylvania, the county seat of Coyne County.

LISTING

Fire is the origin of stone.

—Anonymous

It was no surprise that in those days after the murders, while we dealt with the familial shock of our grief and suffering, Charles was nearly butchered.

Fired by news headlines and television accounts, the public was whipped into a rage. Two innocent children and their mother had been preyed upon in the most ghastly way. "We were worried about a literal lynch mob," said District Attorney Graham Stone, "So we bumped up security."

As Charles was being transported from Florida to Pennsylvania, a large crowd gathered at the county courthouse. The extradition team arrived in Countytown at three in the morning with Charles in restraints. Stone well remembers the media vying for position, the angry mob, a hundred or more people screaming at Charles, "Monster! Look what you've done!" He remembers the voice of one elderly woman screeching again and again, "Fry him! Fry him!" One newspaper carried this phrase as a headline.

I, too, considered Charles a beast, a demon. In fact, he was a smallish, soft-spoken boy, but I thought of him as a fiend; I could not even say his name.

During the first five months following the murders, I was engaged in a practice I now call *listing*. Listing everything horrible that had happened in the preceding months, primarily the murders. But there were other items on my list: family problems, business problems, career problems, emotional problems, hormonal problems. Caught in a negative emotional spiral, I felt our family was under siege. This came from my long held view of "Them and Us"–predators and victims, self and other. I forgot the grace of Thich Nhat Hanh's phrase, "If you are not there, I am not here." I easily fell back into the role of victim.

"We're in a whitewater time, and all we can do is keep our feet in front of us and our butts down," Philip and I were fond of saying.

Frequently, though, I was steeped in darkness, caught in the dread of the drama, suffering more and longer. I lived in fear and wanted retribution, wanted Charles to feel pain. Most of the family felt this way. Unanimously we did not want him executed, but not out of idealism or pacifism. We wanted him to suffer behind bars, to suffer long and hard. For the rest of his days, we reasoned, he should look into the face of what he had wrought.

Mark said, "We want him put away so he can never do this again, to anyone." Three months after the murders, Charles Grand went on trial. The District Attorney was in a highly eager state since this was the first case in his jurisdiction where DNA evidence figured as a deciding factor in a charge and arrest. When Charles stopped the trial on the first day by confessing to all three murders, he had probably been advised by his court-appointed lawyer to do so to avoid the death penalty. The end of the trial was a huge relief for our family. Thank God, we would not have to go through the interminable days of a capital trial, reliving the crime, looking into the face of the killer, salt rubbed into our wounds. The judge gave Charles three consecutive life sentences with no chance of parole. A conviction, however, is not the end of any story. As survivors of homicide, we felt no such thing as what the media calls "closure."

A court advocate—a counselor from the National Organization for Victim Assistance (NOVA)–telephoned our family to offer counseling. One of Connie's four sisters, Dee, the one who had stayed with us in that long-ago summer, was drowning herself in alcohol. We feared for her life and her sanity. I tried to convince Dee, to no avail, that she should see the NOVA counselor. But not one of us was distanced enough from the trauma to seek or accept help. It was all too fresh. I never once considered seeing the NOVA counselor myself.

A RAG OF LACE

Death is not the greatest loss in life.
The greatest loss is what dies inside us while we live.

— Norman Cousins

Death is a rag of lace. One moment you're breathing; the next moment your breath goes out for the last time. I left no journals or poems from those months in 1990, even though I have compulsively recorded everything of note in my life for the last forty years. I could not face a newspaper, watch the TV news. I could not bear the truth. Hearts in our throats, my poor grieving daughters, Lily and Rachel and I could only sob and despair.

The murders left us numb, especially Mark. I could see during the early months afterwards that he was barely ambulatory, only able to put one foot in front of the other. We all seemed to be walking through water–Mark, Lane, Philip, Rachel, Lily and me, not to mention the other siblings from Mark's larger family, Allen and Bobby's grandparents,

Connie's mother, Hazel, the church community and a huge host of friends. It did not help that the murders were quickly captured by nationwide media as top of the evening news, as four-inch headlines in the tabloids.

Connie, Allen and Bobby were only murdered once; our family lived the agony again and again. Painfully and repeatedly, we came to know how it is to live in a family that has suffered a high-profile crime. At the funeral on a perfect autumn afternoon, there were photographers hiding behind trees.

Three caskets in a ghastly row. Who were these children cut off from life so soon, these tender blossoms under a madman's blade? Who were they really? Where did Connie come from and where did she go? What kind of a universe produces such twisted acts? From my early enlightenment experience in the alcohol rehab, I knew absolutely of the existence of a Great Peace. Still, I believed this peace would come from somewhere outside of us. So I went for help outside of myself. I threw myself on the mercy of my self-help group and attended Quaker meetings. I cried and I cried. They held me. I was lost in sorrow. All we were left with were our torturous questions and deep despair.

I dreamed of a gun in the hands of a boy child. It was a toy gun, but to the child it was real. In my dream, I was keeping my aspiration not to let others kill. As I attempted to wrest the gun from the child, I awoke in a sweat. The boy who murdered my family had grown up with an arsenal in his house. The seeds of violence are all around us.

BECOMING FIRE

Become a fire to burn away avarice and self love.

— Ko Un, *Little Pilgrim*

There was more. Throughout the desolate winter following the murders, if I was not angry with the killer, now in prison, I was angry at the culture at large. If I was not angry at society, I curled inside myself, turning the rage inward. My back was frequently in spasm. I took refuge by overdoing everything. I bled at odd times. Mostly I felt a well of despair and confusion so deep that I felt nothing could ever take it away, not even my work.

One sunny January afternoon, I got a call at the home of a client. It was our housemate. "Something's wrong with Philip...choking. He started to get into the van, but, I pulled him out of the driver's seat. Now I think he might be having a stroke." I flew home in the car at about 80 mph on winding country roads, risking my life and others. By the time I arrived, he could not walk or talk. I called 911. I knew he was near death. We stayed on the phone until the EMTs arrived. Philip passed out. The medics strapped him to a stretcher, snapped on an oxygen mask. Riding in the ambulance with him, I screamed over the noise of the oxygen machine, "Don't die! Don't die, Philip! I love you!" The murders and all our life's stresses had taken their toll on his very breath. The ER doctors explained that Philip had suffered a life-threatening asthma attack. They ordered bed rest and a regimen of new medications, together with frequent monitoring at our family doctor's office.

To help with finances, because there was no sick pay for his job driving children with autism in a school van to special programs—and he was often out sick during this period–we needed a Plan B. So in addition to my regular teaching, I made artist's books, small works of art made in the form of books, to sell at a local gallery and in Soho in New York. While I could not bring myself to write at the time, I could spend hours in solace, cutting and gluing, choosing special handmade papers and beads and cords to fashion my miniature books. The pages were blank.

We coped in our various ways. Connie's thin, ethereal voice came to her brother Mark, telling him not to despair, that she and the boys were okay, that they were out of their suffering. Mark and his wife Lane consulted a psychic named Willow who was relaying "messages" from the dead family. The psychic, a single mother, with her five children, actually moved into the murder house. I was appalled, and felt Mark and Lane were being used and duped at a time when they were incredibly vulnerable. But

I restricted my feelings of anger and indignation to intimate conversations with Philip. Our younger daughter Rachel withdrew from the womb of the family. She began to suffer frequent urinary tract infections. Somehow, I felt responsible. If I were a better mother, she would have turned toward me instead of away from me. Connie's sister Dee drank. As our family's unofficial "feeler," I sobbed in my room for hours on end.

My old coping mechanisms, learned from years of drinking and not telling even myself, came to the fore. I threw myself body and soul into work and the busy-ness of daily life. I denied the murders and the culture that spawned them. I shut them out. I thought up a way of putting anonymous anti-war poetry into hollow trees and in potted plants on people's porches and in the box at the bank teller's drive-through window and in plastic bags thrown into the river. That is how I spent my free time in the months after the murders. I was crazed with activity, obsessed with my immature notions of peace.

TRIAL BY FIRE

Tua res agitur, paries cum proximus ardet.

*Your own property is concerned when your
neighbor's house is on fire.*

—Horace

Following is a paraphrase of two articles that
appeared in major US city papers in March 1991:

Student Goes on Rampage, and the Law Looks for Answers

*[MARCH 27, COUNTYTOWN, PA] It was hard to
believe that Connie Starr and her two boys were stabbed and
bludgeoned to death in their separate bedrooms. Why on earth
would anyone want to harm this wholesome, benign family?*

*And how could the person arrested and charged as the
killer have been the boy across a street lined with Colonial
homes on prim acre lots? It strains the imagination. What
had happened to turn nineteen-year-old Charles Grand
from model student to cold-blooded killer?*

In a quiet Pennsylvania courtroom early this month, Judge Jesse Garth attempted to parse the tragedy.

Charles Grand admitted his guilt to all charges against him—the murder and rape of Connie Starr, 42, and the murders of Allen, 17, and Bobby, 14; as well as the theft of a Chevrolet Lumina and several household items.

The decision fell to Judge Garth, after hearing the outline of the D.A.'s case against Grand, whether the nineteen-year-old would die by lethal injection or spend the rest of his life in prison.

This was not the usual trial of a mass murderer. Usually such an event involves contest after contest in a war of wits among attorneys on both sides. The order of events advanced with all due speed, since there was no jury to convince. Only occasionally did the judge interrupt to corroborate the facts. This was a trial naked to the bones, the courtroom hushed in the wake of three horrible deaths, and one man sitting in judgment.

Garth quietly ordered exhibits rearranged to block Starr's family from viewing the most gruesome evidence—kindly masking the procedure as just another bustle of legalities.

Observers found it unusual when the judge stepped down from his bench to get a closer look at witnesses. Here was a first sign that Garth was casting about for a way to fathom exactly what had happened that night.

Grand, still as a stone in his seat, was evidently unmoved as his brutal acts were one by one sharply outlined, labeled, ordered and numbered. He seemed unperturbed as his former girlfriend and whistleblower, Leeanne, 17, told of his return to their Florida motel room with Connie Starr's car and her bloodied shoes and socks. The girl remembered that Charles had given her a fact by hair raising fact account of the murders. Why would she listen?

"Why not?" she replied. *"When someone kills some-one, you want to know."*

On the last day, Grand's cold demeanor broke only when a retinue of his teachers was called to the stand. He bent over in his seat and in slow motion covered his face with his hands.

Man Spared by Judge for Three Hideous Killings

[MARCH 17, COUNTYTOWN, PA.] –Mass mur-derer Charles Grand will not die. Grand, 19, will not die because his record was clean. He will not die because he was psychiatrically compromised when he stabbed and hammered his sleeping neighbors and friends—three of them—to death October 15. And he will not die because he has admitted the crimes, ruled a Countytown Court judge.

In a muted courtroom packed with citizens, Judge Jesse A. Garth failed to order the death penalty, claiming the law provides more of a basis to imprison Charles Grand than to end his life. Yet, he said, the former honor roll student is *"totally capable...of the most heinous indescribable crime that we can imagine."*

Clearly baffled, the judge begged for the missing piece. What in the world motivated this bright and soft-spoken young man from a decent home in the suburbs to carry out such a heinous act? What was the missing piece not uncov-ered in three days of testifying witnesses and psychiatric examinations, by officers of the law, by legal and medical professionals?

"You can almost always find some explanation," said Garth, as he scrutinized Grand. *"This is one of those rare, rare instances where there is no explanation, there is no reason, there is no motive."*

This is "almost like something out of the Lord of the Flies or A Clockwork Orange, stated Garth.

As though still trying to penetrate the impenetrable, the judge said to Grand: "I have no doubt that something is going on in there. This doesn't just happen....We can go to the moon, we can circle Mars, but we don't know what goes on in someone's mind, someone who would commit crimes such as these."

Grand was silent and implacable, looking directly back into the eyes of the judge, and only occasionally casting his eyes downward. When asked at an earlier point in the trial if he had anything to say, Grand answered only with, "No, Your Honor."

His sentence came down only one day after the lineup of witnesses for the defense describing Grand's swift downward spiral in one year from a bright, diligent, enterprising student to a cold-blooded hatchet man.

Ridge High School teachers told how Grand morphed seemingly overnight into a solitary, brooding, unkempt delinquent who walked out of school for good only three weeks before his slated graduation. "I was totally dumbfounded when he told me he was going to quit school rather than serve his detentions," stated Ridge Assistant Principal Timothy Ward.

His inconsolable mother Trina Grand tearfully described Charles as a "smart, bright little boy" who took science fair honors, chatted easily with grownups, worshipped his dad and would sooner "break an arm than miss a single day of school."

Half a year before the crime, he began letting his hair grow long, quit his college scouting and took up with a different group of people. She said he "started hating his family, hating the house, hating everything in it. What happened? I don't know."

According to Trina Grand, Charles called his mother at home hours prior to the murders, saying, "You don't understand. I cracked a couple of months ago."

As his mother continued to weep on the stand, Charles finally broke down, covering his face, sobbing and heaving. According to officials, this was the only time since his arrest that Grand showed any feelings.

"When you say he's emotionless, that's not always true," his mother said. "Look at him now!"

Psychiatrist Raymond Smith used the metaphor of an onion to explain Grand's feelings, which he said are hidden under so many husks of protection that they are impossible to locate.

"Grand suffers from a borderline personality disorder, manifesting in unstable relationships, impulsive behaviors and flare-ups of extreme anger, suicidal tendencies and a complete lack of affect," claimed Smith, who interviewed Charles Grand two times over three months. "Grand reported no feelings of wrongdoing, sorrow or abhorrence after murdering his friends across the street."

"His attitude might be described as holier than thou," added the psychiatrist later. "He said he considered his lack of feelings or guilt superior behavior."

Smith reported that Grand began his strange odyssey last spring, shrieking at his parents with "fire in his eyes" and later brandishing a knife at his father during an argument. While watching the slasher movie, "Friday the Thirteenth," Charles was reported to have remarked about the killer in the film, "He's almost as crazy as I am."

Twice more following TV shows about whales and dogs dying, Grand is reported to have said to his father that he could kill another person, but never an animal. "His father said he got the heebie-jeebies," Smith said.

When his parents made an effort to get psychological treatment for Charles, Smith said, "Charles told them he knew he was crazy, but that he did not believe in psychologists." His parents left it at that.

Judge Garth urged Smith for more. But the doctor admitted he honestly did not know what caused Grand's illness or what, or who, led him to murder.

Our family was satisfied with the verdict. We did not want Charles to die: we wanted him to remember.

What was not brought out at the trial was the fact that Charles was on a crime spree before he committed the murders. According to court records, the Starr murders were planned as a rehearsal, as Charles told Leeanne, for the murders of his own family. They would be next, he told her.

In private, Countytown District Attorney Graham Stone told me there was general speculative agreement among those on the case that "something had gone down" between Charles Grand and his father, Stan. I well remember that before he knew it was his son who had killed Connie and the boys, Charles's father was the one neighbor willing to be interviewed by the media. All the other neighbors were frightened into silence. But it was Stan who said to the TV reporter, "Believe me, we'll get whoever did this. We have guns and dogs."

Hatred begets hatred. It is easy to see that the commission of such acts is possible only in an atmosphere of violence, in a culture of violence that feeds on violence. The slasher films and television shows Charles watched are available to everyone everywhere. Is it true that youngsters who attempt murder or suicide are trying to deal with the loss of those whom they thought were supposed to care for them but did not? And why did Stan Grand need an arsenal in his house?

FIRE ON THE HOME FRONT

As I burnt in the spirit, see, I burn in you

—Rilke, from his last poem

The year of the murders was a year of everything for me: family trials, intimate emotional and physical struggles, the children growing away from home. "The holidays were dreadful," I wrote to my novelist friend, Joan Colebrook. "Arguments with my parents at Thanksgiving and the return of old feelings of worthlessness. Lily, my older girl, broke her arm in two places while visiting here over Christmas. She fell on our ice-covered driveway on New Year's Eve. She underwent general anesthesia to get the arm set, a complicated break made more so by the fact that she's a nursing mother, and that baby Lucy has never been without her.

"Still at age 47, still trying to please my parents, I try to please my children as well. I handmade all Christmas gifts for the family, taking on far too much, and then when Lily broke her arm and Rachel tried to help out by caring for the baby, Joan, I was left with a house in total ruin, running about cleaning up after them. After the baby's bath, I would walk into the bathroom and there would be towels and dirty diapers strewn about, the water still in the tub, rubber duck floating next to used washcloths, oh God! And I, jaw set, teeth tightly clenched–cooking, cooking, cooking copious amounts of food. Lily was so helpless that we had to put the baby to her breast and even make air space for the child to breathe. In the midst of this, I had been making my feeble attempts at writing. The children ran up a phone bill we could ill afford, the food bill was monstrous. At this point, everyone was in foul humor.

"Philip and I are thinking of the Peace Corps, as in 'getting some peace.' We have already arranged for someone to move into our house and care for the dogs this summer. P's still working on his play and on a chapbook of poems. I'm trying to modify my poetry ms. for the Cleveland State University competition. Am finishing *Morning Meditations for the Married*, as well as writing a column for Abbey Press's *Marriage & the Family Magazine*, still writing for *Nouveau* and *The Christian Science Monitor*. Now teaching as well.

"Besides the residency I have coming up at a local school, an after-school arts program for kids has requested I teach an eight-week playwriting workshop for elementary school students which will culminate next year in the annual school play. I'm inspired by Vermont's Bread & Puppet Theatre (Do you know of them, Joan?) to construct papier-mâché masks and have the children write accompanying dramatic vignettes, which they can act out with the help of balloons, kites, the huge masks and home-made, invented musical instruments. Two more books of my students' poems are coming out this year, for a total now of four books....

"Philip sends his love, too. He had a nasty muscle difficulty in his neck the other night, and was in quite a bit of pain. A heating pad solved the problem. We'll keep you posted, darling."

My pathetic letter to Joan was full of pain, pain and more pain. Busy-ness, busy-ness, busy-ness. I never did get to what was really bothering me.

SIT DOWN AND SHUT UP

*The Buddha gave us very effective instruments to put out
the fire in us: the method of mindful breathing, the method
of mindful walking, the method of embracing our anger, the
method of looking deeply into the nature of our perceptions,
and the method of looking deeply into the other person
to realize that she also suffers a lot and needs help. These
methods are very practical, and they come directly from Buddha.*

–Thich Nhat Hanh, *Anger: Cooling the Flames*

For perhaps two years, Philip and I had been
attending silent meeting for worship at our hun-
dred-and-fifty-year-old Quaker meeting house.
In the silence of meeting for worship, I could no
longer deny my feelings. I was forced to look for
solace, look for answers to existential questions that
stemmed from our family's collective anguish. The
stern maternalism of the Quakers comforted me
when I was with them, but most of the time I was
still knee-deep in sorrow. I felt a kind of guilt for the
murders, an intrinsic sense that my family and I had

done something wrong. That we were somehow culpable. In my self-help group and in meetings, friends were sympathetic, even empathetic. Yet in the most secret place inside of me, I felt almost as if we were all in a way *getting high* on grief. Indeed, I experienced my grief as an altered state. Thus, I stacked guilt upon guilt. So many heartfelt hugs from well-meaning family and friends. But nothing sufficed. My long-held notions of safety had been shattered. A part of me had been erased.

A dear Quaker friend called to invite Philip and me to a Monday night lecture in Oldtown, sponsored by Pendle Hill, a Quaker study center west of Philadelphia. She told us the speaker was an American Zen teacher who calls herself a monk, apparently complete with shaven head and black robes, recently returned after twenty-four years of living in Japan. We accepted.

By Monday night, news of Patricia Dai-En Bennage's exotic looks had preceded her, and Oldtown Friends Meeting House was packed. The room smelled of old wood and cloves.

Standing like a mountain before her still audience, Dai-En shone. The light bounced off her fair bald scalp creating a halo. Her Zen robes were multi-layered, full to the floor, elegant, black. Here was an echo of Dr. Brown from the Church of the Savior in Cleveland Heights—black robes, shining bald head and all—a light from my childhood. What lends this woman such presence and grace? I wanted to know. Perhaps her former life as a ballerina. Or is it Zen itself? Whatever that is.

In her poised and practiced voice, Dai-En told her audience that in Japan the Soto Zen monks sleep, meditate, eat and study on the same two-*tatami* [traditional Japanese grass mats that measure about three feet by six feet] meticulously lined up on a raised platform in a long row. This meant that almost their entire existence was played out in the same eighteen square feet!

"I was trained by a recluse Rinzai Zen master I encountered during a pilgrimage on the island of Shikoku. The Shikoku pilgrimage takes about three months on foot if one does not dally. "I hand wove my thongs out of straw and wore the traditional white pilgrim's uniform. I carried the official pilgrim's staff equipped with a bell, which doubles as a walking stick for circumambulating the rocky, mountainous island coast on foot." I was enthralled. I held my breath in admiration.

For centuries, the citizens of Shikoku have offered gifts and food to religious pilgrims whom they identify by their white jackets. Following in the footsteps of Kobo Daishi, the ninth-century Buddhist priest who brought Buddhism from China to Japan, Dai-En set off on Shikoku's circumference—a total of 1,450 kilometers. Some still believe that those who make the pilgrimage to all eighty-eight temples will have their wishes fulfilled.

Today most pilgrims travel by bus. Not Dai-En. Perhaps it was good old Pennsylvania determinism mixed with a dash of her balletic discipline that inspired her to set out on foot. On Shikoku she sought her true teachers, the first of whom she found in the renegade Rinzai master, her recluse teacher Noda Daito Roshi, who taught in a converted school bus-cum-zendo between temples #82 and #83.

"Right off the bat, my master posed three conditions, if I wanted to become a monk: 'Sit down, shut up, and live on alms for ten years.' I lived near his bus in a large, overturned soy sauce vat. He was relentless about policing my sitting meditation practice. I would hide, cowering in the outhouse, but he would never leave me alone. This was far more than I had bargained for. Banging on the old metal door of the outhouse, he would yell, 'Come out! Get out here! I know why you're in there!' It was a living hell. At those times, all I could do was cry. For solace, I would hug the rough, smelly necks of the resident goats." And then she closed her eyes and wrinkled her nose in a sign of extreme distaste. She was irresistible.

Later, Dai-En was sent by her teacher to train with another master, this time a woman–Shundo Aoyama Roshi, chief priest of a training temple for female Soto Zen priests—with whom Dai-En remained for the bulk of her training. There Dai-En lived a 2500-year-old way of life in an ancient temple near Kyoto. She rose at 4 in the morning with only twelve minutes to put away her bedding, go to the bathroom, brush her teeth, wash her face and get to the meditation hall. This was only the bare beginning of a long, strenuous day in the unheated temple. Later Dai-En told me in private that at one point during her training, she almost died of malnutrition. What does it take for a person to believe in her path so deeply that she is willing to risk her life?

Because she had a heart for the Way, Dai-En immersed herself in temple life. She studied the Japanese tea ceremony–even though I knew nothing about it, I had always had a romance with the tea ceremony–and the art of flower arranging. She became fluent in two languages: Japanese and classical Chinese, both written and spoken. A cultural anthropologist, she eventually distinguished herself as the first woman and the first foreigner in Japan to graduate the advanced teacher training of the Soto Zen sect. Her dharma name of Dai-En, she told us, means Big Circle or Big Nothing. When she tells it she always giggles.

Part of the program that evening was a brief dialogue between Dai-En and Jim Thomas, a Quaker/ Buddhist pacifist, formerly a scientist on the Manhattan Project. Jim spoke eloquently of Quaker silent worship, of a Quaker's "descent into the Light," of what he called "radical waiting in silence."

Dai-En immediately countered with, "In Zen there *is* no waiting: you sit, you drop yourself, and you are right in the middle—paradise. "All we need do," she told us, "is to become mindful of the greatest gift we have, and that gift is our breath.

I was impressed. This sounded like instant coffee.

At the end of her talk, someone asked Dai-En to give us a sample of her daily vows. In a deep, almost masculine voice, she chanted in English the Four Great Vows for All:

Sentient Beings are numberless; I vow to save them all.
Desires are inexhaustible; I vow to extinguish them.
Dharma gates are boundless; I vow to enter them.
The Buddha Way is unsurpassable; I vow to reveal it.

I was caught up short. This was beginning to sound like dogma. I reacted by thinking, "Well maybe *not* so instant, this Buddha Way." Still I wasted no time negotiating a path to the front of the room to stand in the line of well-wishers and ask if I might spend a few days with Dai-En in the Allegheny Mountains. My state of mind at that moment was similar to the time I walked up to the wheelhouse in a sweet daze of whale sightings on the Stellwagon Bank in the North Atlantic and asked the skipper for a job. There are times when you know a thing is right.

Without hesitation, Dai-En agreed. I passed her my notebook, turned to a clean page, handed her a pen and asked for her address and phone number. She hesitated, her eyes downcast. She did not want to waste the whole fresh sheet of paper just for her address and phone number—a rare response from an American, a response that stayed with me.

I wanted, no needed, some relief. There is a dynamic in our marriage–one that remains to this day. I leave for two to five weeks, and Philip stays home. Part of our dynamic is that he initially rejects the idea, then later relents. This relationship loop exists, we suppose, because of what he affectionately refers to as his abandonment issues and my engulfment issues. It was my grandmother who bequeathed me the getting-away-alone gene, a longtime habit in her own relationship with my grandfather. I learned getting-away-alone as a child when I could only go so far as the first branch of the cherry tree in my back yard. Lucky for me, Philip is essentially a hearth and homeboy who relishes keeping the home fires burning.

I wanted some relief from my agitation and desperation, and Philip knew this well. He realized the sacrifices I had made during his time of sickness and bed rest. This time he did not hesitate to say go for as long as you need to go.

HAIR ON FIRE

Time is the school in which we learn;
time is the fire in which we burn.

–Delmore Schwartz

Mt. Equity Zendo is a dwelling place for meditation which, during a leave of absence from Japan in 1989, Dai-En Bennage began single-handedly in her mother's living room. It was one of nine rented apartments in a 194-year-old three-story greystone and timbered Quaker manor, Mt. Equity, in the Pennsylvania village of Pennsdale. By the time I arrived, Dai-En had rented a separate downstairs apartment adjacent to her mother's. Some years following my first visit there, the whole mansion was dedicated as Mt. Equity Zendo Jihoji, a Soto Zen Monastery, a frequent stopover for monastics from Japan. In May of 2005, Dai-En was installed by her teacher and "took her seat" as abbess.

I found I did not have to camp for days outside her temple door before the master let me in, as do the novitiate hopefuls in Japan. For this I was grateful! It was spring in the mountains. The cattle were shedding their winter coats. Jack-in-the-pulpit and trillium dotted the surrounding woodlands. This was the first time after the murders I had reached out for specific help with my grief. Thus I became Dai-En Bennage's first overnight student in America. But I was not yet ready to tell her my tragic tale.

I arrived with a lot of baggage and make-up and jewelry, a gift of white rice–I soon learned Dai-En eats only brown rice–and very little understanding of what she meant when she said that in Zen there is *no waiting*.

Later she told me, "When you first arrived, your hair was on fire." I loved the poetry in this, but was not sure of her meaning. This might have been a mild Buddhist rebuke. "Your house is on fire" can mean you are enslaved by your cravings. Or perhaps she was referring to the old Zen saying, "Sit as if your hair is on fire," meant to encourage practitioners. Fire or no, I was full of questions. Yet most of the time we existed together in silence, as in a monastery. So I was forced to sit with my questions. Or I would save them up for Socratic sessions to which I brought my written queries:

Why the rituals?
Name a religion without ritual.
Quakerism.
Why the robes?
Buddhist robes, originally made of rags,
denote the vow of poverty.
Why the shaven head?

> *To symbolize relinquishment of all*
> *attachments, including marriage.*
> Why such a straight back?
> *To allow the lungs and belly their full breath.*
> Why the Buddha statue?
> *The one who bows and the one who is*
> *bowed to are equally empty.*

About the only thing that I felt was empty then was my brain. Even as she demonstrated how to sit, how to hold one's back straight and how to breathe the breath of the Buddha himself, I heard in my psyche a deep warning voice, a male voice: "Thou shalt have no other gods before me!" it boomed. I well remember my early Bible lessons, from Exodus, the plight of Moses' people of Egypt: *Thou shalt not make thyself a graven image, or any likeness of anything that is in heaven above, or that is in the earth beneath, or that is in the water under the earth; thou shalt not bow down to them.*

When I told Dai-En about hearing The Voice, she smiled and asked without a trace of irony, "Shall I put the Buddha in a drawer?"

"That won't be necessary," I muttered.

Still I asked myself how to get rid of the creepy Biblical voice, my Puritan guilt I suppose, from ages of Anglo-Saxon blood remembering. There was no moment when this feeling was resolved once and for all. The Biblical voice gently faded away in the ensuing day after day, week after week, of turning and returning to my breath.

My favorite thing about Mt. Equity Zendo was the pace. Time slowed. The exotic statues, the strange and lovely scents of the incense, Dai-En's deeply ingrained Japanese ways, her use of gesture and facial expression rather than language to convey meaning, her habit of keeping her eyes downcast–which I later learned is called "custody of the eyes"–so as not to be deterred from one's focus, all of these kept me engaged. I drank in these new ways. I inhaled them the way I used to suck up alcohol and smoke cigarettes. So strong was my need for relief from my suffering and so strong the sense of *deja vu.* Somehow I had already been here–not in another life—but in this one. I was experiencing a time out of mind, a turning point, a sense of belonging, not to Dai-En or to Mt. Equity Zendo, but to Zen.

The mornings were full of ritual and what seemed like endless hours of sitting *zazen,* or in meditation. Dai-En explained the meaning of the Manjushri statue she brought from Japan and set at the entrance to the meditation hall. "He uses his sword of wisdom to cut through the bonds of delusion," she said. His wisdom, Dai-En's wisdom, while accumulated from years of practice, was clearly innate, not something gathered from books. While she did give me reading material, such as sections of the *Shobogenzo,* a huge volume by Dogen Zenji, (1200-1253) the primary Soto Zen ancestor, she warned me "Not to read anymore than you sit. Don't gobble the dharma."

Breakfast was meditation. Lunch was meditation. "Let us exist in purity like the lotus," she chanted in a low monotone, to remind me of the purity of the splendid bloom that springs from the mud. Through hours of meditation, perhaps I was beginning to realize a kind of love could actually stem from murder. No matter what, I clung to the notion that the murders were somehow a call to love. But the notion of forgiveness had not yet entered my mind.

One day Dai-En's frail, elderly mother beckoned to me with a bent finger. With child-like eyes and with a sense of secrecy, she took me by the hand into the bedroom in her apartment. She removed a photo from the bottom drawer of an old painted bureau. The room smelled of violets. The photo showed Dai-En as a ballerina, Dai-En with waist-long, thick, straight blonde hair. "Do not tell her I showed this to you," she whispered. "She would not approve." I smiled, covering my mouth with my fingertips. She was beautiful, with or without hair. In this way, I was made by the mother to feel part of the family.

Hours and days went by in slow procession. Afternoons we often devoted to work practice, yet another form of meditation. Dai-En invited me to the nearby country Quaker meeting house to rake leaves to make way for spring blooms: *samu,* work practice. She showed me how to "vacuum" the rug with a broom. I had never vacuumed a rug with a broom: no noise, each stroke a breath, a meditation. She asked me to write a poem or song about my experience at Mt. Equity. It is always a good idea to ask a writer to write something. Later, I learned about a tradition in Zen of writing enlightenment poems. I wrote this, with a tune that sounds suspiciously like a college fight song:

Dark the shadow of the pine made by the moonlight
Deep the river of our souls winding to sea
Buddha the treasure that you give to me
Deep the pleasure of your company, Mt. Equity.

The song was composed to be sung three times, to include each of the three refuges of Buddhism: *Buddha, Sangha (the congregation)* and *Dharma (the sutras or scriptures, and teachings)*, through changing the first word in the third line each time it is sung. Many of my gripping questions had vanished or become less important in the wake of conscious breathing. It was clear to me as I sang that I was falling head over heels into Zen.

After the raking of the Pennsdale Meetinghouse yard, Dai-En and I walked the mile or so back to Mt. Equity. Our walk was punctuated by old pickup truck horns and occasional waves from local farmers (Hey, Patty!) who had always known this woman in robes as Patty Bennage. Back at the *Zendo,* she led a short version of the tea ceremony for Pat and Eli, two members of Pennsdale Meeting, and me. Dai-En had told me about this couple ahead of time—that they serve her one-dish meals at their bare bones home, and that they supply her with homemade beeswax candles from their own hives. This impressed me, as Philip has always said bee-keeping is an esoteric practice, a kind of cooperative alchemy of turning flowers to honey–a sort of white magic with an unspoken spiritual agreement between the Queen Bee, the worker bees and the beekeeper.

In Dai-En's hands, the bamboo whisk moved like a hummingbird's wings as she whipped the green ceremonial tea to a froth. It was a finely powdered *matcha* from Kyoto. In 1991, the green powder would have fetched about fifty dollars an ounce here in the States. There is mostly silence. We're seated on the floor. We contemplate the cup and murmur our compliments to the potter. Breathe in, breathe out. The tea smells and tastes like grass–that is, the lawn. Breathe in, breathe out. We notice the feel of the glaze of the cup on the palms of our hands: where it is a bit rough, where it is smooth, where there are thicker or thinner walls. We gulp the tea ceremonial style, which leaves me dizzy. My heart pounds, reminding me slightly of a marijuana buzz or too many antihistamines. The tea ceremony, like all things here at Mt. Equity, helps me locate my own heart.

NO SELF AND OTHER

The fire which enlightens is the same fire which consumes.

– Henri Frederic Amiel

I don't know why I feel so instantly comfortable with Pat. Maybe because after tea she takes me aside, whispering, "As her first overnight student in America, Judith, Dai-En needs you as much as you need her." I just had not thought of it this way. Then in a whisper so only she can hear me, I unaccountably blurt out to her part of what I have been holding back about the murders. I feel like something inside of me is boiling over and the lid's about to blow.

Now in a conspiratorial voice while Eli and Dai-En walk outdoors, Pat unravels her own secret— the grisly story of her own father violently murdering her mother and then committing suicide. She had already grown and left the household, but the emotional impact was grave. "It's an open wound for me," she said. And how did I relate! "But in Zen, there is no self and other," Pat tells me. I am silenced. I think of Connie and Allen and Bobby. I think of Charles, their murderer. They are never far from my consciousness. I accept what Pat says—that Zen tells us there is no self and other—to mean that she and I have much in common. Yet I know there is more to this feeling. But what? That we both have experienced family murders, yes. But what else?

"I have not yet forgiven him," she tells me.

My heart is pounding. I feel emotionally full up, but pleased to bond with Pat in this strange way. I am overwhelmed at the responsibility of being the first of Dai-En's overnight students, and pleased to be the fresh page upon which Dai-En would write her teachings in America. This is big. Framed in silence, everything feels monumental. But I do not understand this no-self-no-other business. Not at all. I am not a murderer! Or am I?

Later I spy, on Dai-En's bookshelf in the study, a black and white photo of her and her teacher, Abbess Aoyama Roshi at the Vatican standing next to none other than the Holy Father himself. I begin to gather I am in important company. An honor, to be sure, to be personally taught by this joyful and advanced-in-practice woman!

The air is laced with the woody scent of moss garden incense. Dai-En hands me a copy of her book, *Zen Seeds,* which she translated into English from her abbess' Japanese. She asks for my opinion of her translation.

"I only wish I'd been introduced to Thich Nhat Hanh's (pronounced Tick Not Hahn's) teachings sooner, that I had read his books before translating this one. His style is so clear and approachable. I want to know if you think my book will be accessible to Westerners."

I wonder, *Why does she want my opinion? And who is this Thich Nhat Hanh?*

PLAYING WITH FIRE

*How will you survive the kitchen? Make it through the fire?
One key I found is not to calm my mind first and then look
for virtue, but simply to look for virtue. There it is. What you
look for—you'll get more of it.*

———Edward Espe Brown

Although she adores eating, Dai-En does not like
to cook.

"Cooking's one of my passions," I told her
proudly, glad to find a way to be useful, to please the
teacher.

In retrospect, the scene's hilarious. She was in
her study nearby. I was out in her kitchen, slinging
pots and pans, slamming cupboard doors, stomping
around, slapping down the broccoli and chopping
with gusto. Probably at that point—concerning my
training–Dai-En realized she had her work cut out
for her.

She seized on the chaos in the kitchen as a
teaching tool. In a hush of robes, she padded to

the kitchen—one does not wear shoes in a Japanese household, even in America, and even if a monk—and cocked her head around the corner. I looked up from my ardent chopping.

"I thought you'd like to know that the *tenzo,* or kitchen master, is second only to the abbot in a Zen monastery."

I did not get the significance of this comment at that moment. Tenzo schmenzo! It did not stop me from sounding like a bucket brigade on my way to making a simple sesame-rice gruel. This porridge—which includes the leftover rice and some veggies–was topped with a pickled *umeboshi* plum, a yummy Zen staple Dai-En introduced me to for our 7 AM breakfasts. But we sat down to breakfast only *after* enduring two hours of meditation, chanting and ceremony.

And breakfast is not simply breakfast. It is also recitation of sutras. It is a way of sitting in one's chair. It is prayer. It is eating meditation. Or might I call it gulping meditation? I thought this woman consumed her food way too fast. Later I was to learn that for whatever cultural imperative, fast eating is a must in Japanese monasteries, and everyone is taught to finish eating at the same time.

Dai-En and I were an unlikely pair—she in her robes and under-robes and I in my bangles and makeup. Each day, each task was a teaching and a meditation. She reminded me to focus on my breath. To relax my shoulders and my belly. To leave my jewelry in the drawer, to cover my elbows and knees. Even when I retired to my room, she handed me a stick of redolent incense, "for inspiration."

"Don't intellectualize the teachings," she said. "Let them settle into your body. Do not read more than you sit," she repeated. She assured me that she had learned more from her teacher's back than from all the sutras. I watched her back, her impeccable dancer's posture. I wondered if Zen had made her perfect.

She introduced me to a beautiful and difficult passage in *Refining Your Life from the Zen Kitchen to Enlightenment,* by the great Soto Zen master Dogen Zenji, in which he outlines the duties of *tenzo*. "Peel the grapes as if they are your eyeballs." Such care is suggested here that I feel like a mindfulness infant:

> *Keep your eyes open.*
> *Do not allow*
> *Even one grain of rice to be lost.*

I was beginning to learn the elegance of one-thing-at-a-time, of refraining from banging the pots and pans, of dropping some of my ego baggage and allowing my breath to lead me. While mostly I found myself in knee pain or neck pain or back pain in trying to sit on a cushion on the floor, I did experience moments of bliss. I remain supremely grateful to Dai-En Bennage for those early, joyful teachings in *Zen as a practice,* not as a chapter in some book.

Dai-En gave me a second gift that profoundly altered the course of my life. One afternoon at Mt. Equity when we were both tired, she handed me a tape, the voice of Thich Nhat Hanh. I lay my weary body down on the futon in her small guest bedroom. My exhaustion was cosmic. The weight of my life was great. A joss stick burned. From the tape, there came a faint bell sound.

Thich Nhat Hanh was describing how to eat a piece of fruit mindfully. "To eat a tangerine slowly, in perfect mindfulness, is to experience the cosmos with all of its pain and all of its joy firsthand in each bite."

In a prescient flash when first I heard this gentle voice, I knew I would follow this man.

MEETING THE MASTER

"Rabonna!"

– Mary Magdalene, upon seeing Jesus in the garden
after the resurrection.

Dai-En, Philip and I stepped into the auditorium at Hahnemann University Hospital in Philadelphia in the fall of 1991 with a great deal of curiosity mixed with expectation. I carried a bunch of pink carnations for the teacher. This was the first time I was to hear him speak in person, and I was on tenterhooks. Immediately I was struck by his stillness, his elegant composure. He sat center stage without a podium or note. Only once in every half hour during his long talk did he rise ever so slightly from his chair. For two hours, he spoke softly of peace. His language was gentle. I was on fire.

Thich Nhat Hanh (or Th y, pronounced Tie, Vietnamese for master or teacher) is Vietnam's Gandhi. Perhaps his most riveting tale of forgiveness is the story of the sea pirate. In the seventies, he and a few of his disciples sailed out onto the treacherous waters of the South China Sea and the Gulf of Siam to rescue boat people fleeing the Communist regime that had wholly swallowed up Vietnam. In addition to the inherent dangers of the high seas and storms, boat people were prey to pirates who knew they were escaping with their valuables. Thay—Vietnamese for teacher–and his then fledgling monks and nuns encountered a young Vietnamese girl who had been raped by a sea pirate. In his riveting poem, Thich Nhat Hanh writes that he sees himself as the young girl—but also as the pirate. Forgiveness is there for him because his mindfulness is there. There is no separation. He practices and demonstrates one of the Buddha's core illuminations that there is no self and no other. We are not one, but neither are we two. We inter-are.

Nor did he restrict his engagement to the high seas. During the war, he and his students were degraded, shot at, and many assassinated. Thay himself survived an assassination attempt when a bullet missed his head by only inches. Without telling her teacher, one of his first six students in the early period after Thay established the Order of Interbeing (*Tiep Hien*) immolated herself in the name of peace. Members of the Order were denounced as enemies by both sides during the war, yet they all steadfastly refused to take sides. Amid the chaos and gore of combat, Thich Nhat Hanh's monks could not just sit in their temple and meditate. They engaged. They made the battlefield their temple. Dressed in brown–brown for poverty, brown for the Earth– he and his many young followers stepped onto the mine-riddled killing fields, drenched in the scent of rotting flesh, to offer decent, nonpartisan burials. They smeared their faces with peanut oil to block out the stench, but it did little good. Eventually, Thich Nhat Hanh was disallowed by the Communist administration to return to his own homeland. At the time I met him, he had not been back to Vietnam for twenty-five years. Never did he show anger toward his oppressors.

Before I met her, when Patricia Dai-En Bennage first arrived in New York after twenty-four years in Japan, she turned right around and bought a plane ticket for Bordeaux, France, and continued easterly to Plum Village in South of France, Thich Nhat Hanh's home monastery-in-exile. She stayed for three months. There, among voluptuous hills and meadows not unlike those of her native Pennsylvania, Dai-En learned about the "mother Zen" that for Americans she felt would be the perfect foil to the more austere "father Zen" of her own adopted Soto Japanese practice.

We sat eight rows from center stage. There were voluptuous bouquets of gladioli surrounding the small man, who looked even smaller on that grand stage, and two colorful Asian carpets under his chair. And a pretty American woman with long, straight brown hair, Therese Fitzgerald, co-founder of Tiep Hien's lay branch in the U.S., sat on a cushion near the huge temple bell. Two straight-backed chairs were set to one side, one for Thay's Vietnamese dharma sister and longtime assistant, Sister Phuong from Plum Village (now known as Sister Chan Khong) and one for the professor of religious studies who introduced Thay. Five to six hundred people joined their palms and bowed slightly as he appeared from the wing.

Thay punctuated his words with frequent half-smiles and an occasional graceful hand gesture. Every few minutes, Therese invited the mindfulness bell to ring, reminding us all to breathe in and breathe out, and to smile, always bringing us back to our breath.

About midway through his talk, Therese sang a poem by Thay, made up of the following words, which were hand-lettered on a huge banner hung as a backdrop:

IN OUT
FLOWER FRESH
MOUNTAIN SOLID
WATER REFLECTING
SPACE FREE

"We live," said Thich Nhat Hanh, "but most of us are not alive." He told the story of Meursault, from Albert Camus's *The Stranger*, a dead man condemned to death. Of course, Charles Grand sprang into my mind. My breath quickened. The story goes that in his prison cell two days before his execution, Meursault has a revelation. He sees, really sees, the blue sky through a tiny open window above him, and for his last forty-eight hours, because of this vision, he feels truly alive. "Most of us live, but are not truly alive, for we are lost in our worries and our pain and our despair." Ah yes, I was caught in despair. But here came a promise: "By breathing in and breathing out, we can liberate ourselves from our regret concerning the past and our worries about the future." Could freedom possibly be that simple?

"When your body and mind are separated, you are not available; you are not there. You need only to open your eyes–breathe in and to think of your eyes–breathe out and to smile to your eyes.

"Become aware of your non-pain. Become aware of your non-toothache. Breathe in. Breathe out. This is the first exercise proposed by the Buddha."

His words were a balm to my weariness and pain. I sat up straight in my seat, enjoyed my breathing and listened intently. Since clearly I could not spend the night with Thich Nhat Hanh or prepare his breakfast as I did with Dai-En Bennage, I knew enough to seize the moment and listen, to let each of his words penetrate my heart. There is a transmission that takes place between a true teacher and true student that transcends language and logic. It is like an electric charge. This was happening for me as I sat and followed my breath and listened. I had found my true teacher. I felt myself turning into something of inexplicable value:

"We are trees. Our emotions are above, like the branches and leaves, bending in a storm. Our trunks are just below our navels. Our trunks are strong. So when a storm comes and our branches and leaves are blowing wildly in the wind, we can retreat to our trunks—a strong refuge."

I thought of Charles Reznikoff's phrase: "All the little purposes lost in the great design."

"A tree is more than its branches. We are much more than our emotions. Breathing in, I see myself as a mountain. Breathing out, I feel solid. This can save your life in the future if you practice it every day."

I had always known there was a solid self within me, but somehow my branches and leaves always held sway. I had been caught in my emotions, even though I knew well they were unreliable, that they would lead me down the garden path. I was afraid of emotional snares–afraid I might trip over the edge of the mythical cliff of my feelings; I well recalled the state mental hospital. My feelings were so intense I thought I could lose myself again like that. But here was a direct line to the strength of my inner self. His words resonated in my body.

"Breathing in, I see myself as still water. Breathing out, I reflect things as they really are....

"We have the water in us, if we care to become the water again. Stillness is strength. Breathing in, I see myself as still water. Breathing out, I reflect things as they are. The beautiful moon of the Buddha sails across a sky of utmost emptiness. When the water of the mind is not still, calm, it cannot reflect beauty. We have to calm ourselves so that the truth can break through."

I think now of the water experiments of the Japanese microbiologist, Masaru Emoto–his high speed method of photographing frozen water crystals that have been exposed to various focused intentions through language and writing and thought. After all, the earth and we are made mostly of water. He found what the Buddha taught–that water from clear springs exposed to loving words, such as "peace" and "I love you," show brilliant and clear and beautiful snowflake patterns. We inter-are! The crystals from water exposed to negative words, such as "hate," are incomplete, asymmetrical and dull in color.

Each water crystal is like a child who, when unfairly treated, becomes slumped over and dull. But when treated with love and respect, a child shines. A child becomes her true self. Through mindfulness practice, he seemed to be saying, if we can learn compassion for others, and ourselves forgiving others and ourselves once and for all, we flourish. We, too, can shine, fully formed and luminous.

Had the murderer of Connie, Allen and Bobby been unfairly treated as a child? Had anyone sincerely repeated the words, "I love you" to Charles? Why was he such an outstanding student for sixteen years, and then suddenly a dropout who crept around the back yards of his neighborhood in the dark? We knew this much—he was an only child who had been left alone day after day. Connie had often given him refuge after school. But what triggered Charles to do what he did to his neighbors, his allies, his friends? He must have been like Meursault, a dead man walking. If as they said there were no drugs or alcohol involved, what in God's name happened to Charles Grand?

The teacher continued: "Usually, we do not pay attention to things until they go wrong. We should practice getting in touch with things that have not yet gone wrong. Get in touch with your non-toothache!"

If Thay had said, as my mother always did *ad infinitum:* "Count your blessings," I probably would have been deaf to his words. But did he not have a fresh way of putting things? Get in touch with your non-toothache! I got it! "Each of us contains the seeds of happiness and the seeds of unhappiness alike within. To practice means to select the seeds we want to water."

Was I obsessed with the riddle of Charles? Was I too often replaying the murders in my mind? Yes, probably.

What I did know at that moment was that I res-onated with Thay's teachings: all the lovely meta-phors. Temporarily, I was a poet in heaven. He even spoke of the collective consciousness, which seemed one and the same as Carl Jung's collective uncon-scious, what I had always thought of as strictly a psy-chologist's domain:

"Be careful not to water the seeds of suffering in yourself, in others, and in the collective conscious-ness. We are what we think. And we are what we eat, what we ingest. So it is for the problem of diet: to look at what we are eating every day. The same is true on the level of our psyche. What are we putting into it? What kinds of toxins do we ingest every day?"

For me, it had been the toxins of hatred and fear of the boy who murdered my family. I had taken all the poison of my life and poured it into that one person—and now, in a subtle way, Charles was kill-ing me, too. I was ready for a new and different perspective—and this was it! What the teacher said next would stay with me forever: "If you remain a human being, how could you plunge a bayonet into the belly of another human being? You would have to become a beast. You do not feel the vibration of a person you kill, because you have become part of the machine, the war machine. For the next war not to happen, we have to live in such a way as to reduce the daily toxins we take into ourselves and into our culture, reduce and transform them."

Yes, Charles Grand was a beast. Not a flower. A beast.

"When a soldier pulls the trigger, he is motivated by fear. It is kill or be killed."

Was Charles motivated by fear? Fear of what? And of whom? I hardly heard the rest of Thay's talk that evening. When it was over, Sister Phuong sang to us in a voice that made me sense I was in the company of angels. I presented her with my then slightly limp pink carnations. I wanted to fall into her arms and sob. I felt like Camus' protagonist. For perhaps the first time since the murders, I had seen, really seen, a patch of blue sky.

TURNING POINT

*The source of our salvation lies in
what we feel is damning us.*

–Patricia Dai-En Bennage

There was no sure moment when I left behind my despair and arrived at the finish line of equanimity. There *is* no finish line. Clearly I must be a student of the gradual school of enlightenment. Yet, there was an instant when perfect peace in the face of danger, pain and despair became a possibility. That was the day I finally decided to tell Dai-En about the murders.

It was during one of our informal interviews. Dai-En had entertained two guests for morning meditation. I was obliged to wait until they completed their social niceties, and while she stood like a tree at the door with joined palms as they drove away—a custom which seemed to take forever. My face flushed in anticipation.

The exquisite scent of the Japanese incense mixed with freshly snuffed candle smoke filled the apartment. Outside the spring sun shone. I was emotionally loaded. I had awakened with the notion to finally tell her my story—not only the story of the murders, but also the story of how I did not understand what was happening in my life *in toto*—my story of alcoholism and recovery, Philip's recent brush with death, the murders—all of it.

We repaired to Dai-En's study to sit in chairs, thank goodness, as I found cushion-on-floor a constant challenge. The rustle of robes. A long silence, punctuated only by my quick, short sighs. As an ex-smoker I still sometimes had the habit of holding my breath and then suddenly letting it out in the face of anxiety.

"I have something to tell you," I began. Dai-En listened quietly while I unraveled my ghastly story which ended, of course, in tears.

Her first response: "The source of our salvation often lies in what we feel is damning us. We need to know that 'awfulness' is there—and certainly you do—but a key to our practice is how to let *other than* the 'awfulness' in—how to 'eat our tangerine.' Be totally present," she said. "There are no addresses for heaven and hell. They both exist in the mind." My mother had told me this many years before.

Yes, I could see the murders happening again and again in my mind, endlessly rewinding, replaying.

Then Dai-En offered me a classic Zen image that would come to be of utmost help, the one I would tuck in my pocket and pull out hundreds of times over the years to come:

On the cliff, with a tiger above him
And a tiger below him
The Buddhist eats his strawberries.

While I did not then recognize this moment of tears and incense as a turning point, looking back, I now know it was. The tigers are swiping and snarling, and the Buddhist is a monk, a woman. Dai-En had handed me the present moment on a silver platter. While I was still unable to eat my strawberries in equanimity, I began that instant to see this as a possibility, not in an abstract sense and only for the enlightened, but possible for me. Once again, as poet Mary Oliver said, "I felt myself turning into something of inexplicable value."

LIGHT BEYOND LIGHT

When fire is applied to a stone it cracks.

—Irish saying

Hardly could we ignore the karmic implications of the arrival of a Zen priest in our small village. After all, Dai-En Bennage's Mt. Equity Zendo was a two-and-a-half-hour drive from our house. Thus, we could only visit occasionally. Our routine included daily meditation sessions in a corner of our bedroom, and the ritual use of a small bell to bring us back to our breath. Just when Philip and I needed a little encouragement in the first year of our householder meditation and mindfulness routine, something wonderful happened: the exotic Genro and Yayoi appeared.

Genro Lee Milton and his colleague Yayoi Karen Matsumoto moved to our hometown to host predawn meditation. In the early nineties there were few Buddhists for miles around. Genro (pronounced with a hard '*G*') is a Rinzai priest and dharma teacher in Japanese Zen, former residential director of the New York Zen Studies Society Inc., in New York City, and currently abbot of Endless Mountain Zendo in Stillwater, Pennsylvania. He is and was devoted to seated meditation practice as much as anyone I have ever known. The same can be said for the striking Yayoi, who has since been ordained a Zen nun. At that time she had a rich mane of black hair.

At the local health food store, I found their flyer inviting folks to join them for *zazen* at their small garden apartment on Mechanics Street in New Hope. We could hardly believe our good fortune. Philip and I felt a karmic boost, a universal "yes!"

We met the couple for meditation and especially admired their devotion to the practice. While Dai-En Bennage was a celibate priest, we learned that in some Japanese Zen sects monks marry, or, as was the case with Genro and Yayoi, take a life partner.

Philip and I began setting our alarm for 4:45 AM, tumbling out of bed, brushing our teeth and washing our faces, fumbling into our clothes, sleep-walking to the garage and driving the five minutes to join them at 5:15 each morning–except Saturdays and 8 on Sunday mornings–for an hour of chanting practice and seated meditation. (To this day, Philip and I take Saturdays off to laze in bed and take what we call precious time.) At Genro's meditation hall, we chanted in Japanese. Just as in Dai-En's *Zendo*, we wore loose and muted clothing with no jewelry or perfume, clothing fit for a sanctuary.

During chanting, Genro's *basso profundo* voice vibrated in my sternum. I felt my heart open, my mind and body calm, as day after day we repeated the dawn wake-up and the ride in the dark to a room with an oiled pine floor and incense burning on a stark, plain altar. In nice weather, Genro flung open the French doors that led to the garden. Serenaded by bird songs and the occasional garbage truck, we sat in silence.

For Westerners, "finding one's seat" can be dicey. Yet one cannot sustain a practice without it. At first the long sitting time was difficult–not for Philip, whose half-lotus posture is easy and natural–but for me. One bad knee, injured at a retreat where I (not the teacher) forced myself to sit for one week in a modified half-lotus, prevented me from finding comfort in that position ever again. My feet would constantly go to sleep, my one knee ache. When I tried to stand, my feet buckled, and more than once, I fell. Time and again, I struggled with the hour-long sessions, having to remove myself mid-meditation from the cushion to a chair, until Genro gave me the gift of a lifetime. One morning, he presented me with a large wooden sitting bench built by a friend of his–one that no one was using at the time. The bench allowed me to raise my torso and take some of the pressure off my knees. Genro showed me exactly how to sit in a kneeling position on the bench with the tops of my feet on the floor. I did not mind the stretching of my ankles the position requires. It took some practice to feel solid rather than tipsy on the bench, but soon I had the hang of it. Thus, the bench became for me a happy middle way between cushion and chair, a benchmark. I sewed a cushion for the top of the bench, covering it in black cotton. Remarkably, I discovered I was able to sit relaxed and in comfort for almost indefinite periods. Thanks to Genro's gift, almost a year after Philip and I began our daily meditation practice, I had found my seat. I still use it today.

Without even knowing it, Yayoi, too, taught me so much. She grew up the daughter of a Japanese tea master, Matsumoto Sensei, in a childhood home where well-known Zen masters routinely visited. So Yayoi is almost genetically programmed to move with grace in the zendo. The way she serves tea, her offering of tea to the Buddha, allowing the space for the sound of the tea poured into the cup, the way she bows–taking time, taking to herself the Three Refuges: Buddha, Dharma and Sangha, one with each bow–her style of sometimes remaining seated during walking meditation, her elegant chanting of the Buddha lineage–all of these I came to cherish and emulate.

As each day we chanted the Heart Sutra in sonorous Japanese, my brokenness slowly began to mend. Often I felt filled with a new clarity and sense of purpose. On the days when we not only joined Yayoi and Genro in the mornings but attended two-and-a-half-hour evening meditations, I fairly floated through the hours. Gravity had no pull on me. I completely understood the longing for monastic life. I was actually looking forward to sitting in silence and doing nothing! The horror of the murders was abating. A deep peace was taking root in me.

At the time, Philip and I owned our public relations firm. We began assisting Genro and Yayoi with press releases for days of mindfulness and longer meditation retreats. I served as big sister in the meditation hall, which meant cleaning before and after services, reminding people to make their donations, adjusting the temperature of the room, and so on. I also began cooking for retreats.

Philip and I attended our first retreat led by Genro, consisting of 13-hour days of meditation. At a *sesshin*, one does not read, write, watch TV or chat. Even sleep becomes a meditation. Held in an empty borrowed house in a suburb of Philadelphia, ideal for the inner and outer space meditation requires, the retreat was well-attended. On each of our cushions Genro placed a beautifully hand-calligraphed name card. The altar was breathtaking in its simplicity: a single rosebud or buttonwood leaf placed just so. The space around each bud or leaf became a metaphor for the new space inside of me.

In the spaciousness and silence, my pain bubbled up to the surface.

On the third day of the retreat during one of the morning sessions, I found myself face-to-face with all I had ever done to hurt others, intentionally or unintentionally. At the same time I was confronted once again with the accumulated hurt–the murders and multiple wounds that others had inflicted on me in this lifetime. My body and mind were utterly swept up in open wounds and anguish and self-hatred and remorse. I began to cry. My crying quickly escalated to sobs. Mortified, I tried not to audibly sob. I was loathe to draw attention to myself since there were perhaps ten other meditators in the room. But there was no stopping it. Innocently, I had not thought to bring tissues–being still new at this–and my nose and eyes ran copiously, continuously. My stomach convulsed. The meditator next to me assumed I was suffering an allergy attack. In a whisper, he offered me a decongestant. I declined. It was January, and huge icicles hung from the eaves, dripping in the silver light outside the window. I, too, melted.

When it came time for my formal interview with the teacher, I was unable to quell the tears. Haltingly and with great difficulty, I explained to Genro the depth and magnitude of what I felt was happening inside of me. With this teacher, I felt free to express the depth of my grief in intimate ways I had not been able–or ready–to tell Dai-En.

"Good," he said. "This is good. You're doing very well. Now stay with the pain." Oh God, I thought. All right. But I'm not sure if I can take this. All the self-hatred and grief is here with me now–my alcoholism, the abortion, the murders.

The man was encouraging me to feel pain? Revolutionary! Always before I had tried to push discomfort away, to make it go away with alcohol, cigarettes, food, incessant activity. On that day, my tears and Genro's words cemented the foundation of my liberation from the trauma of the murders. Traditionally, I had been taught ways to squelch–or fix–my shadow side. "Your emotions will lead you down the garden path" was the notion I had inherited from parents and well-meaning others. "Throw the bottle in the trash and think about it tomorrow." Here, at the age of forty-something I was given permission to feel those not-nice emotions. On that day I also learned my pain would not break me. Next, I discovered what lives on the other side of hell.

During my suffering meditation, "...with the passion put to use in my old griefs...." as Elizabeth Browning once put it, I continued to sit with the pain. I learned that the pain would not break me. Or was I indeed breaking open? As I sat deep in my misery, there was no way to know. I found myself descending still, impossibly further into the abyss of suffering. My mind and body felt like they were made of glass. But strangely, they were of one piece! Suddenly, the next moment, light broke through the darkness. Suddenly, my body-mind was huge. I was made of love. Suddenly, and inexplicably as I sat on my borrowed bench in an empty, borrowed house in the Pennsylvania winter, I felt a fresh peace, a place of sunshine within. Inadvertently, I had taken another step down the road to forgiveness.

Soon after this retreat, Yayoi and Genro learned that their landlord had decided to move into their apartment, and that they would be forced to find another place to live and practice. In the meantime, they had already scheduled an eight-week Zen class and accepted donations from ten students. Philip and I offered our office–the largest room in our farmhouse–for the full eight weeks. They accepted. Philip and I began inviting others to share our morning meditations. Genro formally dedicated the space as a zendo. Thus, Old Path Zendo was born. We moved the cushions into the office, and there they stayed.

ROMANIA: OLIVIA AND THE MINDFULNESS BELL

The stars were only sparks of the fire which devoured us.

—Elie Wiesel

Dai-En advised us not to go to Romania. She did not feel we were ready for the depth of suffering we would encounter there. It was 1993, two years after the murders. Philip and I had been accepted by the Peace Corps for an assignment to the Seychelles Islands, but were unceremoniously turned down at the last minute due to Philip's childhood allergy to sulfa drugs. Disappointed but undaunted, we applied for a private humanitarian assignment to Romania. The time was a mere four years post-Ceausescu, the country's despotic Communist leader, who had been executed in what became known as the Romanian Revolution.

Repeatedly I recited my mantra: *the murders are a call to love. A call to love.* I felt charged to make sense of the tragedy, and to do so with my own life. As Philip and I deepened our study of Mahayana Buddhism, we discovered the *bodhisattva ideal,* or a way of life devoted to others. Our impulse to join the Peace Corps, and finally find a way to be of use in Romania—these were paths for expanding our love in service to others, for manifesting the *bodhisattva ideal,* a way of walking in the company of angels.

Americans entering Romania for the first time in decades found thousands upon thousands of abused infants and children crowded into unspeakably filthy orphanages. Many were dying. Many suffered withered limbs due to untreated frostbite. Buildings were replete with broken windows and leaky roofs. For lack of love and touch, many of these children exhibited autistic behavior—banging their heads against the bars of cribs where they were jammed three to a bed on urine-and-feces-infested mattresses. These conditions were exposed on network TV, and now the world knew about the orphans of Romania.

Taking Dai-En's cautions to heart but forging ahead, Philip and I took a private assignment for the summer to an orphanage/neuropsychiatric hospital at Paclisa, a peasant village in the mountains of Transylvania. Along dusty roads far west of the capital of Bucharest, we lived in a crumbling Hungarian baron's castle, with a single light bulb dangling from its cord in the center of our high-ceilinged room. With a changing cast of characters—often as many as fifteen visitors—from diverse countries, many from France, we shared a huge bathroom and (mostly) cold shower. Early every morning villagers would lead their cattle out of the town and into the adjoining countryside to pasture. Horse-drawn wagons clattered by. Huge, impassive pigs stood in the dirt roads. Shepherds and flocks dotted the hillsides. Babushka-headed women beat and cleaned their rugs over stone bridges. The men of each village fermented their own plums for brandy. We had to pinch ourselves to remember we were still living in the twentieth century.

In the midst of this earth-born beauty were the suffering children. Ostensibly to teach English through the arts, Philip and I were provided a spare classroom by orphanage officials in which to work with an older group of orphans. Because their heads were shaved, we could not identify the younger kids as boys or girls. More often than not, they were clothed only in shabby underwear which doubled as swimwear in the orphanage pond. Still they were children–innocent and glad.

From the second story, when they caught sight of us walking by, young children would call from the barred windows of Spital Paclisa, "Mama! Tata!" Mommy! Daddy! Each weekday our students, who ranged in age from eleven to twenty-three, would wait quietly on benches in the darkened hall of the school building, sometimes for hours before we arrived, to unlock the classroom door. One of their first acts on meeting us was to gather in the playground and sing *en masse* the only English song they knew, "The Battle Hymn of the Republic." Then they rendered it in Romanian–these beleaguered cherubs, their voices a chorus of need. That was the first time our smiles gave way to tears. It was here in the emotionally rich environment of Romania that Philip and I were to plumb new depths of forgiveness.

Dai-En's sense of the enormity of the suffering there was right. If it were not for our inflatable meditation cushions and our daily practice of sitting, we would scarcely have had the strength to go on. Our practice of daily meditation and mindfulness allowed us to endure the unendurable and begin to forgive the unforgivable. For reading material, we took in our bag one small pamphlet–*The Discourse on the Eight Realizations of the Great Beings*, by Thich Nhat Hanh–which we read and re-read aloud in our room at night:

The First Realization is the awareness that the world is impermanent. Political regimes are subject to fall. Things composed of the four elements are empty, containing within them the seeds of suffering. Human beings are... are without a separate self. They are always in the process of change—constantly being born and constantly dying. They are empty of self and without a separate existence. The mind is the source of all confusion, and the body the forest of all unwholesome actions. Meditating on this, you can be released from the round of birth and death.

It was not that we were looking for freedom from birth and death; we just wanted to be able to endure. In this Romanian peasant countryside, it was difficult to realize that a political regime had just fallen. The lives of the peasants were lived close to the land, as always since time immemorial. But had the Ceausescu regime continued, we in the US would not have known of the suffering orphans overseas. We would not have been allowed into Romania, which prior to that was an isolationist country barred to foreigners. Now borders were dissolving. We could see clearly that these children were the same as our own children and our own selves, that we have no separate existence.

The Second Realization is the awareness that more desire brings more suffering. All hardships in daily life arise from greed and desire. Those with little desire and ambition are able to relax, their bodies and minds free from entanglement.

In Paclisa, we had a chance to test our desire for hot showers and fresh whole foods. The food was fatty and inferior. One evening, we glanced into the kitchen to see the cook preparing a fresh fish feast with crisp vegetables and sauces unlike any meal we had experienced at Spital Paclisa. Our daily diet was made up of the food that was served to the children—carbohydrate-laden and vegetable-deficient.

"Who are you cooking for?" Philip asked the cook. "Domnule Director," came her quick reply, eyes downcast. Once home in America, we were told by reliable sources that under "Domnule Director's" management, fifty children had been permitted to freeze to death in an unheated building on the hospital campus. He had burned their slight bodies in the orphanage furnace to keep himself warm. Later in Bucharest, we met some of Mother Theresa's nuns who had rescued from yet another Romanian orphanage fifty infants on the brink of death. We were face to face with a level of suffering we had never imagined.

The Third Realization is the awareness that the human mind is always searching outside itself and never feels fulfilled. This brings about unwholesome activity.

Bodhisattvas, on the other hand, know the value of having few desires. They live simply and peacefully, so they can devote themselves to practicing the Way. They regard the realization of perfect understanding to be their only career.

Many of the children were bodhisattvas. For example, there was eleven-year-old, flashing-eyed gypsy Florin, whose parents had forced him onto the streets to beg for them as a very young child. Florin was a holy child, no doubt about it. When he walked into our classroom, the light around him seemed palpable. He carried a Bible and acted as mediator when fights broke out among the other children.

We will always remember bright-eyed teenager Olivia with the withered hand—Olivia who walked with a limp. One day the children tumbled into our classroom in obvious distress. Fourteen-year-old Claudia, a wan child, wore bandages on her wrists. The kids were out of control, unable to focus. If only our grasp of the Romanian language were better. We summoned Lilia, a translator. She urged the children to sit in a circle on chairs.

Slowly, agonizingly, as she translated, the reason for their agitation came out. Many of these "orphans" still had parents. Many came from conditions of addiction, poverty and despair. Due to Ceausescu's national ban on birth control, supposedly because he wanted to build his armies with youngsters who were early inculcated with his politics, families who could not afford to keep them at home were forced to let go of their children. They were then sent to hundreds of the notorious orphanages.

Claudia was such a child, the youngest of five. Here at Spital Paclisa she was far better off than at home where she would be systematically abused by her parents. Her parents had recently sent for her. That morning, in desperation, Claudia had slit her wrists with a jagged tin from the kitchen. As her story came out, our classroom filled with sobs. The children's pain was cosmic.

Tears in her eyes, Olivia stood. She left the circle and limped across the room to the desk where we kept a small mindfulness bell which we had taught them to ring at special times. With her good hand, she cradled the bell, and with her withered hand, she invited its sweet sound. We all stopped to breathe three slow breaths. In that moment, conscious breathing calmed us all. Indeed, there are bodhisattvas everywhere.

The Fourth Realization is the awareness that indolence is an obstacle to practice. We must practice diligently to transform unwholesome mental states that bind us, and we must conquer the four kinds of mara [temptation] *in order to free ourselves from the prisons of the Five Aggregates* [form, feelings, perceptions, mental formations and consciousness] *and the three worlds* [desire, enjoyment, formlessness].

Clearly, Philip and I had two choices in Romania–practice or go home. We practiced together every morning to the sounds of cowbells and whistles beneath our high window as the cowherds and shepherds led their flocks from the walled family compounds to the hills, and the village farmers–looking as Van Gogh-ish as an actual Van Gogh painting–shouldered their scythes and pitchforks on the way to the outlying slopes.

The Fifth Realization is the awareness that ignorance is the cause of the endless round of birth and death.

Bodhisattvas always listen to and learn from others so their understanding and skillful means can develop, and so they can teach living beings and bring them great joy.

Somebody was always listening in Romania. In a country of 21 million people, there were an estimated ten million hidden microphones. When our translator, Lilia, invited us to dinner at her apartment, we were dismayed to hear her story. Lilia was a teacher at the Paclisa orphanage school. Over months and years, she had painstakingly collected supplies for her classroom—books and pencils and posters—only to have them all disappear overnight, without recourse to or comment by school officials. As she told us her story, Lilia kept the radio volume high and her voice low. We knew why: she was afraid of who might be listening. (Yes, the "Revolution" had happened, but the system was still intact.) Unaffected by the decades of fear that had paralyzed her nation, we were able, with the ears of Avalokitesvara, the Bodhisattva of Compassion, to listen deeply to Lilia's story.

The Sixth Realization is the awareness that poverty creates hatred and anger, which creates a vicious cycle of negative thoughts and actions. When practicing generosity, bodhisattvas consider everyone—friends and enemies alike—to be equal. They do not condemn anyone's past wrongdoings nor hate even those presently causing harm.

We found Romania a land of locked doors, locked hearts. Much of what we encountered in this beautiful country—from dead, abandoned and abused dogs and cats on the grey streets of Bucharest, to the subclass of martyred infants—expressed a vicious cycle of tyranny, poverty and fear. These were the wheels that turned passionate, intelligent, creative people into maniacal, paranoid neurotics. And yet Philip and I remember our time in Romania as among the happiest of our life. For each moment we gave love, love came back to us a hundred-fold.

We brought magic markers, color, song. Air France gave us free shipping for a dozen large boxes of school supplies–most items these kids had never laid eyes on. I will not forget the look of surprise and joy on the face of twelve-year-old Dorel when, for the first time in his life, he held a colored marking pen and began to draw. The children designed a large mural; colors exploded on the walls. They taught us the Romanian alphabet; we taught them English. Ecstatic, they drew, designed and created and sang.

Philip carried from Pennsylvania a huge donated electric keyboard with an adapter. Each day he would play, and each day we would raise our voices together–"It's a Wonderful World," "Kumbaya," "Amazing Grace." Songs that stir. The children sang to us their haunting Romanian *doinas,* folk songs which we recorded and played back to them. We taught them how to sing and dance "The Hokey Pokey." Again and again, they would beg us: "Meesuz Toy, Meestair Toy, Hawkey, Pawkey, Hawkey Pawkey!"

When the superintendent of schools came for a visit, when he saw the room, he cried for the sheer carnival of gladness that greeted him. Never had he seen such a room full to bursting with the visions of children. In truth, our room looked much like an American primary classroom. The walls were so full of the children's artwork that we had to string clothesline to make a place for the rest. An illustrated alphabet danced on a string, festooning the room with our joys.

The Seventh Realization is the awareness that the five categories of sensual desire—money, sex, fame, overeating, and oversleeping—lead to problems. Although we are in the world, we try not to be caught in worldly matters. A monk, for example, has in his possession only three robes and one bowl. He lives simply in order to practice the Way. His precepts keep him free of attachments to worldly things, and he treats everyone equally and with compassion.

Too soon the summer was over and it was time for us to return to Bucharest, where we planned to take a bus south through Bulgaria to Istanbul. We would have felt greedy to keep our belongings—three suitcases of well made clothes and jewelry—and to leave the children with nothing. So Philip and I devised what we thought was a fair way to give it all to the children, leaving ourselves only the essentials. Afterwards, we worried the items we gave them would be confiscated by orphanage authorities. In truth, they probably were.

Among a people deprived for so long, greed rages. We were confident, too, that the school supplies we had managed to bring along were later sold on the black market to line the pockets of petty officials, the skeleton vestiges of the fallen Communist regime. Soon after, we closed the door to Spital Paclisa and left our bare-bulbed room in the dilapidated castle. We were almost certain the children would go back to school without their colored chalk and crayons and colored paper and tape and brushes and paints and glue and paper clips and magic markers...and the keyboard.

The Eighth Realization is the awareness that the fire of birth and death is raging, causing endless suffering everywhere. We take the Great Vow to help all beings, to suffer with all beings, and to guide all beings to the Realm of Great Joy.

Philip and I took leave of Spital Paclisa in a Wagnerian scene of lament. We moved toward the exit gate with the orphans en masse–the *sanghakaya*, a body of one–weeping children hanging from our bodies. We, too, wept.

Often now, we find ourselves wondering what became of these precious lovelorn children. With no training for life in the outside world, what? But we can do more than endure this sadness. We can endure joyfully. Now we have learned we can contain not only the memory of Romania, but we can contain within our hearts—hearts like the giant samovars we saw in the lobby of our castle—the suffering of her children. Through the practice of silence and looking deeply, our hearts welcome everything.

We forgive—we do not condone. Looking deeply we can see why conditions in Romania had come to its inevitable impasse. We forgive Domnule Director for warming himself at the fire of the bodies of orphans he allowed to freeze to death. We forgive those who probably sold our supplies on the black market. We forgive the passionate people of Romania whose fear in the face of tyranny created countless petty tyrants, toppling ethics and tenderness. Looking deeply, we see that their unskillfullness was passed onto them by generations of their ancestors. We see the people of Romania are not separate from us. For a perfect teaching on this depth of forgiveness, which is really a teaching on non-self, we recall Olivia and the mindfulness bell.

Thus I was brought one giant step closer to forgiving the boy who murdered Connie, Bobby and Allen. Thus my call to love matured.

DOORS THAT SLAM LIKE GUILLOTINES

Be a lamp unto yourself.

—Shakyamuni Buddha

You are the light of the world.

—Jesus Christ

Perhaps I had unfinished business inside prison walls, and that is why I felt a clarion call to go to Countytown, a medium-security men's prison. I went to visit the husband of a Quaker friend who was imprisoned for a far less severe crime than murder—namely, growing marijuana in his attic and selling it, in order to pay tuition for his boys' private schools. When my Quaker friend approached me, saying her husband, Carl, was desperate to resume his Buddhist practice but needed some guidance, I jumped in. At that time, Charles Grand was still alive in a federal prison. Perhaps, although I did not reason this out, visiting Carl was a shallow foray for me into the dangerous waters inhabited by Charles Grand and others like him.

Daniel Berrigan says we should enter the prison as a bridegroom enters his bridal chamber. My first visit to Countytown Prison was nothing like that. Countytown is infused with the odors of fear. Sweat. Dread. Stale cigarette smoke. Lives on hold. Impassive faces of the guards. No eye contact. No expression in the voice. Not a welcoming smile. No windows. Then the emptying of pockets and purses. The metal detectors. Large metal doors slamming. The tension of waiting before four successive chambers with massive doors unlocked by machine and slamming themselves shut like gunshots, like guillotines. Prison doors do not close softly and mindfully. No slam, no lock. Lock clicks into place. Slam says this is final. Slam is part of the punishment.

I was not yet ordained by Thich Nhat Hanh, but I was still a practicing Quaker. All Quakers serve as ministers. We do not hire professional preachers. As a Quaker and a Buddhist, I was finally toning down the mascara and bangles. As a Quaker, I was permitted to enter the prison during non-visiting hours as a "religious counselor." Carl was glad to see a friend—someone he could ask about his kids, how they were getting along. He was ardently interested in Tibetan Buddhism, had once lived in Nepal. He did not mind that I came from another tradition, I offered to sit with him in the visiting room which was more like a closet with a window—while just outside the halls echoed with the ubiquitous slamming doors, booming PA system, raucous yells and mumbled epithets. With prison ambience as the ground of our meditation, we practiced together the posture and breathing that were lately giving me so much relief. I was able to bring Carl some books on Tibetan practice—soft cover only, for in a hardback one could smuggle a blade, or drugs.

We relished our shared silence. Carl began meditating alone in his cell. He began to speak of his jail time as an opportunity to find peace and light, as liberation. After about a year of visits, Carl said, "I'm having some difficulty keeping the discipline without a group—a Sangha—to encourage me." There were no Buddhist services at CTP at that time. I told him I would check to see what the prison would allow.

The Chaplain, it turned out, was Methodist. I explained to him that I combined my Christian (Quaker) and Buddhist (Zen) practice, but that I spring from Methodist roots, am ever grateful to my Methodist forebears for giving me a strong sense of devotion to God, the sacredness of place, the poetry of the scriptures. I explained that my husband, also a Quaker and Zen student—with Southern Baptist roots–did not want me to lead the group alone, so he committed to come along. We planned a weekly mindfulness practice class of an hour and a half. After a meeting with the Deputy Director of Treatment, who was enthusiastic–"This could be big; it could be really big!"–we began with a poster:

Still the Mind and Open the Heart
Mindfulness
Meditation

Breathing
Posture
Seated Meditation
Chanting Practice
Walking Meditation
Readings

Thursday Evenings 7-8:30
With Judith Toy, Quaker and ordained Zen monastic And
Philip Toy, Quaker and Zen practitioner for 27 years,
Founders of Old Path Zendo, New Hope

I swallowed hard when I wrote the words "Open the Heart," as frankly, I still harbored a prejudice: the stereotype convict is a hardboiled thug who might scoff at the idea of opening his heart. But I wrote it anyhow and am glad I did, because ten guys signed up for the first night of mindfulness practice!

There were forms to fill out and an orientation session on prison rules for me. For example, "There are to be no 'favors' done for inmates. This jeopardizes the integrity of the Volunteer Program." That was tested on the first night when an inmate asked me to carry out a letter for him; I had to refuse. It was clear that Jane, administrator of the treatment team who showed me the prison ropes, held a genuine affection and respect for her men. The system for calling the men up, even when they hold passes, does not always work. So there were only four men that first night with Philip and me. Carl read a passage from one of Chogyam Trungpa Rinpoche's books on Tibetan Buddhism. We shared sitting meditation and walking meditation.

I'll never forget the gardenia that night. A dear friend had brought me a fresh gardenia to place on our altar at home. Unaware that "botanicals" were considered contraband at CTP, on a whim we took the creamy flower with its waxy green leaves and laid it on the table in the small, stuffy meditation room. Its fragrance served as our incense: we knew *actual* incense was a no-no.

I felt chills as some of the men told us they had known Charles, one of them at Ridge High School, several from the early days, when he was held in Countytown. Calypso, in a voice like a cement mixer, shared with us that he was a Vietnam vet, that he had committed countless atrocities. Because of this, he told us, he had suffered deeply and continuously. He often became obsessed with thoughts of homicide or suicide. But he truly wanted to put the war behind him and find peace. How was this man different from Charles Grand? Yet there I was with Calypso, offering the teachings of peace.

Absorbed by the prison sounds as the context of our practice, we discovered inner harmony in the power of the group. As we made ready to leave the prison that first night, we passed the gardenia around our meeting table. Each man inhaled its sweetness, touched its tender petals and leaves. I snapped a mental photo of Calypso with his nose in the flower: Calypso and the Buddha, Calypso and the Christ. I can still smell that gardenia.

Nevertheless, even as my fear of entering the prison began to abate, I had my bad days when it was not high on my list of destinations. The recliner and the TV beckoned. Or, as the sun set, my eyes wanted to close. I often resisted the routine that required Philip and me to walk through the metal detector again and again, or subject ourselves before the days of airport security to the handheld detector, arms outstretched. "It makes me feel like a criminal!" I complained. Sometimes en route in the car, Philip and I bickered. Yet without fail, once we had been in the prison for a time practicing together, our minds lightened and we always left walking on air.

Steven was a student of Satya Sai Baba. When we told him that the father of one of the men in the group—Deepak—had also been a disciple of Sai Baba, Steven asked to join us. And he stayed. It helped that a friend from Old Path Zendo Sangha came along, and when Philip and I moved to North Carolina, Steven protected the prison sangha by staying with the men in our stead.

Most touching was the friendship that developed between the two sanghas—Old Path and the Prison Sangha. Here was a friendship between folks who never met in the flesh. The men dedicated their practice each week to Old Path Sangha, and at Old Path Sangha, we dedicated our practice to the inmates. We never asked the men how they happened to be convicted. We just sat. We just walked. We just smiled. We just beamed out our love.

We continued the custom of taking a flower and passing it around before saying goodbye. Deepak developed a habit that led to the naming of the prison sangha: as we passed the flower around to the men each week he would pinch off a petal, or a fragment of a petal, and file it away in his pocket. He stowed the sweet-smelling bits in his cell as reminders of our times together, as a token of Mother Earth. Later we learned that the floral fragments were seized as contraband by the guards during a lock-down. They were certainly mistaken for drugs. Deepak told us the lock-down was worth it, and he continued to pinch petals. Such was his longing for what these small fragments symbolized — earth, which the inmates saw so little of, its flowering, peace, acceptance, new life. We couldn't find it in our hearts to deny him those petals.

Thus the prison group was named by the men: *Serene Lotus Petal Sangha.* At the end of each meeting, there were goodbye hugs all around.

TO LAY MY DRAGON DOWN

A little komodo lay down its sweet head.

— thepoormouth.blogspot.com

Four years after the first time I met Thay, there was standing room only at the Cathedral of Saint John the Divine in New York City, where Philip and I attended his teachings on love–a birthday present from my own beloved. It was October 9, 1995, and I had just turned 52. The acoustics in the cavernous nave were challenging. Nevertheless, these teachings were to have a strong influence later on my ability to forgive.

In addition to freelance writing, I offered home-schooling parents a resource room at our house at Rolling Green Farm. To celebrate the Chinese New Year with our students, on this trip to New York I had purchased a large dragon puppet at a Chinese grocery store. Along with my fears, frustrations and attachments, I had lugged the big dragon box into the cathedral. I had no choice. We planned to catch a cab and return home after Thich Nhat Hanh's talk. Thay's nuns and monks chanted the name of the bodhisattva of compassion. I kept my palms joined during the recitation, which was quite long. My arms ached from carrying the dragon box. But by then I had practiced long enough to simply notice, "Oh, my arms ache." By then I was more than ready to lay my dragon down.

After the long chanting, the crowd's heightened anticipation was palpable. "Nothing has come from nothing," Thay began. "From nothing, you can get something." I noticed his voice sounded strained. Even Thay gets nervous, I thought. There were thousands of people hanging on his first words. And outside there were still long lines slowly snaking into the cathedral.

"This sheet of paper was born at a certain time. Before that, it did not exist, but if you touch the piece of paper deeply, you will find that our idea of birth is wrong. When you touch the piece of paper deeply, you touch the sunshine. If you could remove the sunshine from it, the piece of paper would not be possible." When Thay says the word, "touch," which he often uses, he pronounces it "t-uh-sh," with a slight French accent.

"When you touch the piece of paper deeply, you touch a cloud. The whole cosmos is present in this sheet of paper. So we have to reconsider our idea of birth. The true nature of the sheet of paper is no-birth and no-death. There is only transformation and continuation in this sheet of paper. If the sheet of paper is not born, it cannot die."

"We think we can assassinate people and reduce them to nothingness, but this is not possible. I will ask this young monk to burn this piece of paper to try to reduce it to nothingness. [The young monk sets the paper on fire. It burns.] Some smoke has gone up to the sky and become part of the cloud from this piece of paper. That is part of its continuation. Some of it has become heat; it has penetrated me. It has penetrated you. Our perceptions and our consciousness are like that. Nothing is born; nothing dies."

The term *assassinate* brought Connie, Allen and Bobby to my mind. If they have not vanished, where are they now? Sometimes in my heart of hearts I feel disloyal to them for going on with my regular life. Is this what they call survivor guilt? But now my life was becoming increasingly more true to myself. I had brought into my home my joyful work with children. So the room that doubled as a Zendo became a classroom during the day. The homeschoolers loved jumping onto the stacks of large square cushions, or making them into a boat, sliding around on the oiled pine floor. I poured my creativity into "play-shops" for the kids. We explored various world cultures and learned new languages, sang folks songs, invented exuberant plays.

Later, on the topic of meditation, Thay said: "A wave is always water, and if a wave can touch the ground of its being, which is water, it can transcend birth and death. Likewise, if we can touch the ground of our being, there will be no fear. The ground of being is the love that is always there." Yes, our love for Connie, Allen and Bobby would never die. Is that where they reside? In our hearts? Isn't this a cliché? I was stuck in the words.

During meditation, I was learning to become unstuck from the words, to let the precious language go, to let whatever I was feeling at the moment drop down into my belly. To augment our income, Philip was driving autistic kids to special schools. We were both writing poems. We got rid of one car. I was beginning to see this Zen thing meant eliminating the inessential, paring down one's lifestyle. I began to shed some of myself.

Thay was speaking of an impersonal love–of the capacity and intention to offer joy and happiness, the Buddhist version of the Christian *agape*. Certainly I knew, had known, deep down, almost from the beginning that the murders were a call to love. If they were not to destroy me, I *had* to see them this way, as heat and fire–as a painful teaching on the road to what the sages call liberation.

Considering the sketchy acoustics of the cathedral, and even though Philip and I were obliged to move our position twice in an effort to better hear him, I let Thay's teachings wash over me. His voice, the hundred-year-old sanctuary, my softening heart–all of these allowed me to hear him deeply.

"Happiness can be created and nurtured through mindfulness." This was already beginning to happen in my life at home, as each day we sat quietly, walked quietly and at least attempted to take the practice off our cushions and into our life. It was autumn again. I had never quite seen the luminescence of the colored leaves after a rain the way I was seeing them now. My friends were commenting on my new inner peace. Some of them began showing up for morning Zen practice. We took baby steps of mindfulness.

"Here is a mantra you can use with your loved one," said Thay. "Darling, I suffer. Please help." If only Charles Grand had learned to ask for help! But he was a boy who "fell through the cracks," according to Connie's brother, a high school teacher for forty years. When Charles left school only three weeks before his slated graduation, no one pursued him to find out what was happening. A year later, my family was dead.

"Suffering is caused by misunderstanding and wrong perceptions," offered Thay. I thought then, rather foolishly, of Shakespeare's comedies of error. The mistaken identities. The tangled webs of deception and duplicity. How many times I had lied to impress someone, or to hide my many misbehaviors. Mindfulness gets under your skin. You begin to see your own actions for what they are, sometimes phony and self-serving. But we don't judge ourselves. We simply notice.

"When you get hurt and you suffer, you have to go to the other person and ask for his or her help. A group of people might misunderstand another group of people. We don't want to be the object of misunderstanding or hatred. Happiness is not an individual thing. We cannot have happiness, peace and safety if we continue to be angry. But our heart will be opened the moment we understand the suffering of the other."

How could I or would I ever understand the suffering of a murderer?

Thay went on: "I see that on all of US money is the phrase, 'In God We Trust.'

There is something good and true in every one of us, and if we are able to touch the seed of truth and love in ourselves, we know it also exists in the heart of the other. So you can go to him or her in order to work out a solution."

A tiff in my marriage, yes. Charles Grand? No! At this point I was too afraid to even contemplate communicating with a murderer. In no way was I ready to forgive, nor did I see this as an option.

"In Buddhist meditation, we practice looking deeply. The practice of mindfulness is the practice of being there, calm and deep. The seed is in everyone. It is the Holy Spirit sent from God. The Holy Spirit can be recognized by any and every one of us. Where there is understanding, where there is love, the Holy Spirit is there. We have to learn ways to make the Holy Spirit present in our heart. When you are mindful, you are there. When you are there, you understand; you can love."

Now Thay was speaking the language of my Methodist roots and his words fed me. I determined to buy a copy of his new book, *Living Buddha, Living Christ,* before leaving the Cathedral that evening.

He went on: "If mindfulness is there, the Buddha is there also, because the Buddha is made of mindfulness. If mindfulness is there, God the Father and God the Son are there. When you are present, your heart is open, and you can see the whole cosmos. You are truly there, truly alive." Yes, I was having moments of this aliveness, sparks and flashes of it.

"In our practice we practice mindful eating. When we eat a string bean, we call it 'string bean.' We pick up only a string bean—not our worries and anxiety. This is like the Eucharist; you do everything in the presence of God. And that means the Holy

Spirit is within you. Jesus is there in the presence of each moment. We have to practice being there twenty-four hours a day. We have to practice love twenty-four hours a day."

It was becoming possible. But I was still caught up in my zigzagging emotions. I needed many reminders. Inspired by Thay's teachings, Philip or I would pick up our small mindfulness bell at odd intervals, invite the round sound of it, stop what we were doing and breathe. I also enjoyed teaching the children to use our bell. They loved the bell, would fight over who got to be bell master for the day.

Like so many other children of Christendom, for me the Eucharist had gone stale. As I listened that night, Thay was transforming the rites of Christianity, freshening them, bringing them alive again in my body and mind and heart. His voice was a bell, carrying me back to my roots.

This year was a rite of passage as we prepared our younger daughter, Rachel, for marriage. She had graduated from the University of North Carolina, Greensboro, in December of 1994. That same month, the two of us took a memorable mother-daughter trip in her VW camper to explore the barrier islands outside of Charleston, to scope out a place for her and Dean, her husband-to-be to set up housekeeping. In June of 1995, Rachel and Dean were married at low tide on the beach at The Isle of Palms, South Carolina, in a small homemade wedding that I helped design and produce. And if I do say so, it was a humble masterpiece. They placed a stick of incense in the world's largest incense holder—the beach sand–and we recited the incense offering gatha from Thich Nhat Hanh. In deference to Dean's Roman Catholic family, we substituted the words *wise ones* for *buddhas and bodhisattvas:*

In gratitude, we offer this incense to all wise ones through-out space and time.
May it be fragrant as earth herself, reflecting our careful efforts, our wholehearted awareness, and the fruit of under-standing, slowly ripening.
May we and all beings be companions of the wise ones. May we awaken from forgetfulness and realize our true home.

I appreciate nothing better than planning a sacred event. Like Thich Nhat Hanh who knew he wanted to be a monk when he was ten, I had early aspirations of the holy life. But who ever heard of a Methodist monk? Instead, as a teen I was off to the races with alcohol and cigarettes and sex. Here was a man who had lived my early aspirations–monk, best-selling author. And he spoke the language of poetry and love.

Much like the Dalai Lama, Thay shows not a trace of bitterness about his exile. His answer to the bitter loneliness and longing of exile is beyond for-giveness. His answer to having his country destroyed by the US was to bring to America the gift of the Buddha. I wondered, was Charles empty of a self-powered existence, devoid of a separate self, when he committed the crimes that shattered our lives? If so, what forces had conspired to turn him into a beast?

In the epic of our family, Charles and Allen had become like Cain and Abel. Here was the ultimate betrayal, the taking of one's life by a friend. This was a horror so deep that in the atmosphere surrounding this man's teachings, the horror could only teach me this: if the murders do not consume me, they must be a call to love. To love more, and to love deeply.

To unlearn my anger and rage, I had to look down so far into the suffering of the perpetrator that the suffering of the victim did not eclipse it. But how to love the one who performs the hateful?

On our way home from Thay's talk at the Cathedral, as Philip and I gazed out from the open deck of the Weehawken Ferry, the harvest moon and the midtown skyline were cinematic. We stood close, holding hands. Our breath mingled and went out with the stars and the twinkling lights of the city. I felt a clear sense of relief as I let these words of Thich Nhat Hanh sink into my heart: "It is not enough to suffer." He had struck a match that created a heat that penetrated me. I so longed to lay my dragon down.

ORDINATION

…Being wonderfully together….

–Thich Nhat Hanh

It has never been my way to dip my big toe in the water of a pool; I dive head first into the deep end. After our visit to hear Thich Nhat Hanh speak in New York, I bought and read his book, *Living Buddha, Living Christ,* and I was floored. That this teacher was able to marry the Christian and Buddhist ideals in such a clear and unbiased way seemed like the miracle of Cana. I decided it was my aspiration to become a lay member of Thay's order, the Order of Interbeing. So I approached Dai-En Bennage and asked if she could help.

"I'm not really qualified to mentor you, Judith," she answered. "But I can put you in touch with Lyn Fine, who founded the New York Metro chapter of the Community of Mindful Living (CML), Thich Nhat Hanh's lay sangha there." At the time I had no notion of how the Zen world works. I was somewhat annoyed. Why couldn't Dai-En help me with this? After all, she had recently received the Fourteen Mindfulness Trainings, which brought her into Thay's order! She was the one who started the Zen ball rolling for me in the first place. Nor did I want to travel the two-hour-plus bus ride and expend the energy to start all over again with a teacher new to me.

My aspiration to ordain was stronger than the inconvenience. The trip turned out to be worth it. Lyn Fine was a quiet, petite power-pack of a woman, authorized by Thich Nhat Hanh as a Dharma teacher in 1994, soon after we met. As one of the earlier lay members of the Order of Interbeing, she was able to model for me our teacher's clear and gentle approach. More than that, Lyn climbed on to the *joyful* side of my otherwise depressed Libran scales, stood there, and wouldn't get off until they were in balance again. To Lyn, I owe my original awakening to the middle way.

After meeting her the first time, I willingly began taking the trip to Manhattan to Lyn's vintage high-ceilinged New York apartment near Riverside Drive on the Upper West Side, where she lived with her mother, Lenore. It was a revelation to me that in their personal living space they hosted days of mindfulness, inviting the New York City public into their living room. During indoor walking meditation on those days, I would pass by Lyn's study stacked high with books and papers where she worked on her NYU doctoral dissertation on international education and peace studies. Always by example, she taught me how to chant the Heart Sutra, how to listen to a dharma talk without taking notes, how to practice indoor and outdoor walking meditation, how to use the chanting book, how to invite the mindfulness bell in the Order of Interbeing way.

Lyn often delivered to me one of her love gazes, which one young practitioner dubbed "eye hugs:" a long, attentive look into my eyes—a look that says *Dear One, I am here and you are here, and I cherish you in this moment.* At first I wasn't sure how to return the favor or how to respond. In fact it felt a little gooney. But soon enough I calmed down to return her gaze with the focus and affection she intended. My speech was as direct as Lyn's eyes. I let her know straightaway that I was interested in ordination, which meant I would become a core member of the Order and a lay minister. But first things first—I needed to "enter the stream" by receiving the Five Mindfulness Trainings, the Buddhist precepts, in a ceremony which Lyn was authorized to conduct.

She began visiting our farm–soon afterwards dedicated as Old Path Zendo by Rinzai priest Genro Lee Milton. Philip and I followed Lyn's lead, inviting the public into our home for mindfulness practice. She began coming to our town to lead retreats; she gave her first dharma talk ever at our Old Path Zendo.

In an age-old ceremony, one October Saturday afternoon in 1996, again near the death day of Connie, Bobby and Allen, Philip and I prostrated ourselves side by side, touching the earth as we received from Lyn the Five Mindfulness Trainings of the Order of Interbeing. She gave me the lineage name Clear Light of the Source, and Philip, Flowing

Stream of the Source. Here was my first step toward full ordination:

The Five Mindfulness Trainings are a loving transla-tion of the Buddhist precepts by Thich Nhat Hanh and the monastic community. As a concrete expression of the Buddha's teachings, the Mindfulness Trainings represent a Buddhist vision for a global spirituality and ethic. These teachings embrace the Four Noble Truths and the Noble Eightfold Path, the path of right understanding and true love, leading to healing, transformation, and happiness for ourselves and for the world. We see these trainings as a North Star, or a guide. To study, practice and regularly recite the Five Mindfulness Trainings is to cultivate the insight of interbeing, or Right View, which can remove all discrimination, intolerance, anger, fear, and despair. If we live according to the Five Mindfulness Trainings, we are already on the path of a bodhisattva, one who lives for the sake of others. Knowing we are on that path, we are not lost in confusion about our life in the present or in fears about the future.

Reverence For Life
Aware of the suffering caused by the destruction of life, I am committed to cultivating the insight of interbeing and compassion and learning ways to protect the lives of peo-ple, animals, plants, and minerals. I am determined not to kill, not to let others kill, and not to support any act of killing in the world, in my thinking, or in my way of life. Seeing that harmful actions arise from anger, fear, greed, and intolerance, which in turn come from dualistic and discriminative thinking, I will cultivate openness, non-discrimination, and non-attachment to views in order to

transform violence, fanaticism, and dogmatism in myself and in the world.

True Happiness

Aware of the suffering caused by exploitation, social injustice, stealing, and oppression, I am committed to practicing generosity in my thinking, speaking, and acting. I am determined not to steal and not to possess anything that should belong to others; and I will share my time, energy, and material resources with those who are in need. I will practice looking deeply to see that the happiness and suffering of others are not separate from my own happiness and suffering; that true happiness is not possible without understanding and compassion; and that running after wealth, fame, power and sensual pleasures can bring much suffering and despair. I am aware that happiness depends on my mental attitude and not on external conditions, and that I can live happily in the present moment simply by remembering that I already have more than enough conditions to be happy. I am committed to practicing Right Livelihood so that I can help reduce the suffering of living beings on Earth and reverse the process of global warming.

True Love

Aware of the suffering caused by sexual misconduct, I am committed to cultivating responsibility and learning ways to protect the safety and integrity of individuals, couples, families, and society. Knowing that sexual desire is not love, and that sexual activity motivated by craving always harms myself as well as others, I am determined not to engage in sexual relations without true love and a deep, long-term commitment made known to my family and friends. I will do everything in my power to protect children from sexual abuse and to prevent couples and families from being broken by sexual misconduct. Seeing that body and mind are one, I am committed to learning appropriate ways to take care of my sexual energy and cultivating loving kindness, compassion, joy and inclusiveness – which are the four basic elements of true love – for my greater happiness and the greater happiness of others. Practicing true love, we know that we will continue beautifully into the future.

Loving Speech and Deep Listening
Aware of the suffering caused by unmindful speech and the inability to listen to others, I am committed to cultivating loving speech and compassionate listening in order to relieve suffering and to promote reconciliation and peace in myself and among other people, ethnic and religious groups, and nations. Knowing that words can create happiness or suffering, I am committed to speaking truthfully using words that inspire confidence, joy, and hope. When anger is manifesting in me, I am determined not to speak. I will practice mindful breathing and walking in order to recognize and to look deeply into my anger. I know that the roots of anger can be found in my wrong perceptions and lack of understanding of the suffering in myself and in the other person. I will speak and listen in a way that can help myself and the other person to transform suffering and see the way out of difficult situations. I am determined not to spread news that I do not know to be certain and not to utter words that can cause division or discord. I will practice Right Diligence to nourish my capacity for understanding, love, joy, and inclusiveness, and gradually transform anger, violence, and fear that lie deep in my consciousness.

Nourishment and Healing

Aware of the suffering caused by unmindful consumption, I am committed to cultivating good health, both physical and mental, for myself, my family, and my society by practicing mindful eating, drinking, and consuming. I will practice looking deeply into how I consume the Four Kinds of Nutriments, namely edible foods, sense impressions, volition, and consciousness. I am determined not to gamble, or to use alcohol, drugs, or any other products which contain toxins, such as certain websites, electronic games, TV programs, films, magazines, books, and conversations. I will practice coming back to the present moment to be in touch with the refreshing, healing and nourishing elements in me and around me, not letting regrets and sorrow drag me back into the past nor letting anxieties, fear, or craving pull me out of the present moment. I am determined not to try to cover up loneliness, anxiety, or other suffering by losing myself in consumption. I will contemplate interbeing and consume in a way that preserves peace, joy, and well-being in my body and consciousness, and in the collective body and consciousness of my family, my society and the Earth.

The memories we gathered from those times are precious as breath: Lyn wearing her Mona Lisa smile, always arriving in the zendo with a stack of books and papers and a glass of warm water, to make a nest on her cushion; Lyn's soothing voice as she taught pebble meditation to the children of our sangha; Lyn playing on her recorder the "Nammo Botat Quan Te Am," a chant to Quan Yin or Avalokitesvara, the bodhisattva, or saint, of compassion. One by one at a day of mindfulness, each of us scattered into the garden a few ashes of the body of the son of one of our sangha, Barbara.

Barbara's son was gone. Connie, Bobby and Allen were lost and gone. Genro, our Rinzai priest friend, gave us an auspicious gift–a small concrete statue of Kshitigarba, or Jizo in Japanese, the bodhisattva of great aspiration. Jizo saved his mother from a hell realm, and he is known as a protector of mothers, babies, children and travelers, as well as lost causes. In Japan, entire gardens are dedicated to Jizo, sometimes with one hundred statues where travelers light incense and invoke his name. I wondered if Charles Grand were a lost cause. Could Jizo help? We learned of a ceremony for newly acquired Buddha statues in Japanese Zen practice called "opening the eyes of the Buddha." I asked Lyn if Thay does a similar practice. "Not that I know of," she replied, "but we can invent a ritual."

We carried the concrete statue outdoors and placed it in the pot of a small red maple that we intended to plant in the yard. Mindfully, silently, we lined up to sprinkle water on the statue and the tree, dedicating both at once. I thought of all those who were lost to me–my grandmother, the son of Barbara, a friend who had recently succumbed to AIDS, Connie, Bobby, Allen. It was a hot, humid day. Our shaggy white terrier, Kodo, stood in a strategic spot, lapping up the water from the watering can as we poured it over Jizo.

Lyn continued to stand firmly on the joy side of my scales. Once during the winter rainy season retreat, I was living in a tent for five weeks at Deer Park, Thich Nhat Hanh's California monastery.

Inspired by a custom of our teacher to undertake a ten-day fast during the winter retreat, I decided to try a liquid fast. I have always felt while on retreats that if one eats breakfast, lunch and dinner, too much of one's day is taken up with waiting in line for food, eating the food and then digesting it, while our hours of exercise are fewer. With the encouragement of several monastics, I began planning my fast. I would dedicate it to the 40,000 children of the world who starve to death every day of the year. Surely if I thought of them, held them tenderly in my arms and heart, I would have the strength to continue.

Lyn arrived at Deer Park Monastery with her ninety-four-year-old mother, and we had a happy reunion interview. I told her of my fast and of my intention to dedicate it to the starving children of the world.

"Don't forget those who have enough to eat," she declared softly. "Such as the children we see around us here."

Like Thay, Lyn has always reminded me that it is not enough to suffer. Why should I discriminate between starving and healthy children?

She had this gentle way of mentoring me, meeting me where I am, as if she knew that my nature is not to be pushed. Attending her days of mindfulness in New York City and planning together our weekend retreats at Old Path Zendo in Pennsylvania and later at Cloud Cottage in North Carolina solidified my practice and taught me through action what it means to live simply and dwell in joy.

My true initiation into the Order came at one of the early retreats at Old Path Zendo. That day, Lyn had brought two dharma sisters from the NYC Metro Sangha to our Rolling Green Farm in Pennsylvania. I was once again on emotional overload. Planning and hosting these retreats was energy-intensive. My younger daughter Rachel, who had never truly recovered from the anguish of the murders, was angry with me. Prior to her marriage described earlier, she had decided to leave home with her boyfriend, to live and continue her college career near her sister Lily, in Greensboro, North Carolina. I was feeling deserted by my daughters who seemed to be breezing off to create a Brave New World without their mother and father. I had recently made the decision to ordain. My dharma cup was running over. Both overwhelmed and overjoyed by the large and solemn nature of my commitment, my true calling, and at the same time suffering with old feelings of grief and abandonment, I fell to sobbing. Lyn and the two other lay women from the Order, Marjorie and Monica, scooped me into their brown-clad arms and held me as I cried for perhaps an hour. Or so it seemed. Here was my true initiation into sisterhood. In the dark brown cave of their arms, I was safe. No longer overwrought, I was home. They gave me permission to fully feel what I was feeling with no questions, no interrogations, no judgment and no advice to keep my chin up. They offered no tissues, no glass of water.

Ordination Day finally arrived. It is October 24, 1997. The setting was Omega Institute, Rhinebeck, New York, where at the end of a week-long retreat in the presence of well over a thousand people, thirteen of us–none of whom I had met before–were to be ordained by Thich Nhat Hanh into the Order of Interbeing, *Tiep Hien*. Omega Institute had never hosted this many people. Each of us ordinees had been given a pink carnation to hold in our laps.

I was upset because Philip could not be with me, an issue of money. In fact, several of our Sangha paid my tuition for this retreat. And our daughter Rachel was about to have a baby, any day, any moment. Lyn was there, and it was she who, during the formal ceremony among the monks and nuns in their bright gold *sanghati* robes, read the Fourteen Mindfulness Trainings—the vows we took—over the microphone. Her strong voice was an anchor. Earlier she suggested I breathe with Philip, with Rachel. Breathing in, I offered my love to them, and breathing out, I sent my joy.

Finally, as if in a dream, I heard Thich Nhat Hanh call my name:

"This is to certify that Judith Toy has been ordained as a member of the Core Community of the Order of Interbeing, *Tiep Hien*. She belongs to the forty-third generation of the Lam Te School and the ninth generation of the Lieu Quan Dharma Line. Her Lineage Name is Clear Light of the Source, and her Dharma Name—I was hearing this for the first time—is Chan An Mon, True Door of Peace.

With my ordination, I join a lineage directly tracing back to the Buddha. On my Certificate of Ordination is printed this poem by Thich Nhat Hanh:

The great Way of Reality
Is our true nature's pure ocean.
The source of Mind penetrates everywhere.

MURDER AS A CALL TO LOVE

From the roots of virtue springs the practice of compassion.
Precepts, concentration and insight—
The nature and function of all three are one.
The fruit of transcendent wisdom
Can be realized by being wonderfully together.
Maintain and transmit the wonderful principle,
In order to reveal the true teaching!
For the realization of True Emptiness to be possible,
Wisdom and Action must go together.

FORGIVENESS

*Forgiveness is the fragrance the violet
sheds on the heel that has crushed it.*

–Mark Twain

Death days are difficult. In the midst of the color of each beautiful autumn after the murders, a part of me always reached out, but could not touch, Connie, Bobby and Allen. It was five years after the murders, five years of daily meditation and mindfulness practice. I had learned the Zen trick of using language to go beneath language. Often without success, I aspired to keep space around my words and to maintain wide margins in my life, to write like a Japanese brush painting replete with white space. Look twice, three times, at the master's brush work. Yes, that *is* a chickadee on the branch under a vast reach of cloudless sky! Zen poems, too, are short and sometimes obscured. They grow out of silence:

An autumn evening
Without a cry
A crow passes.

How strong the poet Kishu's emblem of that which is neither silence nor language. Expressed in this spare way, the crow's hushed flight is deeper and more meaningful.

I knew the heart of Thay's practice had sprung from tragedy–the killing fields of the Vietnam War. In one of his best-known poems, *Call Me By My True Names,* he writes:

I am the frog, swimming happily
in the clear waters of my pond,
and I am the grass-snake who,
approaching in silence,
feeds itself on the frog.
I am the child in Uganda
my legs as thin as bamboo sticks
and I am the arms merchant, selling deadly weapons to
Uganda.

That autumn morning my heart was particularly heavy. I picked up a pencil. Turning in the Bible to Isaiah, I found the archetypal imagery I was looking for to write my way out of suffering, to express how homicide is a hideous ritual:

<u>*Make the minds of these people dull*</u>
<u>*their ears deaf and their eyes blind*</u>

so that they cannot see or hear or understand.
If they did, they might turn to me and be healed.
    —The Lord, in a vision of Isaiah, 6:10

A mother and her two sons are dying:
there is blood on the walls
but they do not yet see the Lord
on a high throne, exalted
his beard and robe filling temple suburbia
that awful, lawn-dark night.
They see only stabs of light
as they are raped, hammered, slashed
by the hysterical boy, three flaming
six-winged creatures standing by.
The killer sees no creatures, huge
by the beds, covering the face of the
mother with their wings
covering the body of the bludgeoned son with their wings
now flying up, cradling the younger brother's body
with their fifth and sixth wings, chanting "Holy,
O holy, holy,"
their voices deep and terrible, enough
to warn the boy, stabbing with his hands
stabbing with his legs, stabbing with his penis
enough to squelch his screaming for a second
as he stops, sniffs the gruesome air, and goes on.

To my astonishment, as I wrote this poem, I began to identify with the rage of the nineteen-year-old committing the murders, stabbing and bludgeoning, raping. Suddenly in the act of writing the poem, I seemed to inhabit Charles's body! I felt blind, out of control, out of my own body, out of my own mind. I went numb. Rage was paramount. There was nothing but hatred and stabbing, my beating heart. I had entered a physical affinity with the enemy. But he was no longer the enemy.

As I finished the last line, I was convinced that Charles had been completely out of his body and mind when he killed my family. That was the very day I stopped casting him as a beast and visualized him as a boy in whom something had gone terribly wrong. The pain of my resentment vanished on the spot. Despite my mindfulness practice, for years I had been trapped in fear and blame. Suddenly I understood that he was not a monster, but possibly a good boy who had become–for reasons I will never know for sure–a beast that night. This was not a dark revelation; it was suffused with light, a kind of *bodhi* or awakened moment.

So what I experienced was luminescence, in part a fruit of five years of sometimes very reluctant mindfulness practice. This felt like the shaman's special kinship with fire, heat and light, associated with purity and knowledge. I closed my eyes and suddenly I could see through a tunnel of darkness the secrets of yet another.

I developed an urge to see Charles. Alarmed, a friend said, "Wait. Do not visit him yet. Begin with a letter." I was still afraid even to write the letter. So I began what I could do–the practice of mentally putting myself in Charles's prison cell and holding him tenderly in my arms. I did not associate what I was doing with the Buddhist love practice of *maitri*, but now I know that is what it was. I stopped wasting energy wishing that Charles be punished. Embraced by silence and spurred on through vaguely recognizable, peaceful language, I was now able to feel compassion for him. It was as if a dam had broken, and a nascent forgiveness began flowing in my belly, a river of perfect understanding that might serve to heal my sorrow, grief and rage.

I was not aware of this, but at that time, Charles was refusing to see or talk to his parents, who had essentially become social pariahs, cast out by all of their family and friends for producing Charles, "a monster." Then on January 10, 1998, a Saturday morning, the prison guards failed to make their normal rounds. By the time they found Charles's body, he had been hanging by his neck from a twisted laundry bag for over two hours. When they called his mother, Trina Grand said, "You get him up! I know he's not dead!" It took a while for prison officials to convince her that Charles had already turned blue by the time he was found.

When I learned about Charles's suicide, I not only mourned his death. His death became a trigger of sorts that brought back the horror full blast.

When I began work on this book, I did what I could to find out what might have spurred Charles to take his own life. I talked to the district attorney at length, who told me about the speculation that there was big trouble between the boy and his father. Charles's public defender was bound by the law of confidentiality not to talk with me. With my heart beating fast, I carefully read the court records. I interviewed my first husband, Mark, who had known Charles personally. He told me that Charles must have "fallen through the cracks" at his high school. He was the one who first told me that not long before the murders, Connie had worried over the boy's condition, after he had dropped out of school and was refusing to shave or cut his hair. She sensed he was looking for trouble. Little did she know how he would find it.

Years later, I decided to telephone Charles's mother, Trina. Again, my heart pounded as I picked up the phone. Will she hang up on me? Will she be willing to hear what I have to say? Her hello on the other end was sweet, clear, feminine. I told her whom I was, that I had found a spiritual path and that through daily work on that path I had eventually been able to pardon her son in my heart. I told her about wanting to visit Charles, about mentally holding him in my arms. With a lump in my throat, I admitted to her that before I had summoned the courage to write a letter to Charles expressing my forgiveness, two years had swiftly passed. By then it was too late.

She began to talk and talked nonstop for about twenty minutes without interruption. The first thing she said was, "There was someone else in that house. I'm looking across the street at the house right now. I'm at my window watering the plants.

"Charles said there was someone else in there that night, and the Lord told me he was right. If you had called me three months in the future, you would not have found me. We just put the house on the market, we're moving away and we're going to become anonymous. Charles wrote a book about the other person in the house, and I believe him. Most of the book, though, is about how he grew up. It always made him feel better when he was writing. I think it helped him. But they wouldn't let him publish the book...."

In fact, in a long and cumbersome legal battle, Mark was able to get the law changed in Pennsylvania to bar any convict from making money on personal story book publication.

"Writing always makes me feel better, too," I said, finally locating common ground.

In fragmented, emotional bits and pieces, Trina talked and cried and told her side of the story. None of the people who had been in the Grands' lives prior to the murders remained in their lives. "In twelve years, yours is the first and only call. No one has called. No one!

"I only got to visit Charles once," she went on. "He was behind a glass wall. Then he wouldn't see us anymore, or even speak to us. He refused to shave or cut his hair. He did for the trial, but that was it. He was depressed."

Trina openly shared with me how, after the trial, she had been saved by Jesus Christ. Now, she and Stan were sending money to one of Charles's friends in the prison. Trina said it was a miracle that her marriage was intact. "Stan found the Lord, too," she said, "but he still hasn't forgiven his son. He wants to know this: if there was someone else in the house, why did Charles plead guilty? He can't deal with it and doesn't want to talk about it, ever."

She never mentioned the indisputable DNA evidence found at the scene.

While in prison, Trina continued, Charles fell in love with a woman nine years his senior. They were engaged to marry. I did not ask her how this happened, but the woman was someone on the outside who began writing and visiting Charles. "Then she broke it off with him. She wrote him a letter; it was a love letter, really. I saw it. That was when he killed himself."

But this was not Charles's first attempt at suicide. As late as seven years after the murders, Trina said she had been trying to get the district attorney to allow a lie detector test. The DA adamantly refused. Then the letter from his girlfriend arrived.

"His dreams had been bothering him, and he was deeply depressed," she said. "At least he wrote us to say goodbye. He wrote, 'Just let me go.'"

"Two months after Charles's death, I heard the Lord's voice saying, *Their blood cries out for retribution.* I had to look up the word; I didn't even know what it meant. Then the Lord gave me a reason to go on," Trina remembered. "My mother [the grandmother Charles had intended to murder] needed some special care."

Trina relayed a dream she had: "My husband was playing the drums in church. Everything was white, bright white; there were people in robes, and I could see their hands, clapping, clapping. Charles was coming down the aisle between the rows of people, his hand upraised, and he was saying, 'Praise You, Lord, for everything you've done for me.'

"I wanted to go to Connie, Allen and Bobby's graves," she said in her stream-of-consciousness stammer, "But then I thought to m-myself they aren't really there. I believe Charles and Connie and Bobby and Allen are all together—and they know the truth.

I've been watching John Edwards on TV, you know the way he talks to people about those who've gone on?" She began to cry, and even over the phone I felt the depth of her loneliness and grief. "But my Christian counselor would say it was the devil.

"I can't call you because Stan will see the phone bill. He doesn't want me talking to anyone. But if I did call you, what would be a good time to call?"

Trina did call me once, before she and Stan moved and became "anonymous," but I was not home at the time. I did not hear from her again. I had known that Charles had invented a story about someone else being in the murder house. It was clear to me that what he had done was too horrendous and unthinkable to admit, so in his twisted mind, he invented another person. And perhaps in some way it really was another person within himself. But a real other person would not have the same DNA as Charles. There was no other DNA save that of the victims.

What stays with me from that day is that Trina and I cried together. Without any feelings of blame or retribution or revenge, we were just two women united by the common bond of one horrible act one horrible night in 1990 that permanently changed both of our lives—two women who were able to share love and sorrow as our common ground: two women's tears, born of murder and grief, now called to love.

POST-TRAUMATIC STRESS DISORDER

And taken by light in her arms at long and dear last
I may without fail
Suffer the first vision that set fire to the stars...

                                        –Dylan Thomas

I met Janeen at Wandering Creek, a New Jersey boarding school for deeply wounded girls where I led a regular poetry workshop for adolescents. At Wandering Creek, the girls drank bleach, or cut themselves with pencil lead, or climbed the rose trellises to the rooftops, threatening to throw themselves to the ground. They wet the bed. Their poems tore at my heart:

> *Mom call*
> *me monkey*
> *Mom tell*
> *me tell*

> *me you*
> *tell me you*
> *love me*
> *How much*
> *a lot*
> *how*
> *much is*
> *a lot*
> *call*
> *me monkey*
> *just one more time*
> *let me lie*
> *in my*
> *dandelion*
> *bed*

A loud noise set Janeen off one day and she was suddenly reliving her childhood terrors. In an instant her reality morphed and she was no longer present in her body. Her energy jettisoned off in all directions. Inner pyrotechnics. Her words became jumbled, slurred, run-together, nonsensical, frenzied. The person I knew as Janeen had taken leave of this girl's body. I did what I had been trained to do, attempt to refocus her attention. I took her hand, walked her outdoors and pointed to the sky. She was crying. Softly, I called her name. "Janeen, Janeen, do you see that cloud? I think it's shaped like a dragon, don't you?"

This technique worked, but not right away. Deeply shaken, I could only remember my own flashback as if I had been the murdered—waking, feeling the murderer was crushing my skull with a blunt instrument. I had felt the blows. I knew what she was going through. I called her name, pointed to the sky, repeated the question. "Oh, and look at that one, an angel!" In time, her breathing slowed and she began to calm down as I drew her attention again and again to the fluid July sky, the animate shapes of clouds. It was crucial that I remain calm and still, a lightning rod to her storm. This was difficult because of my own memories that suddenly welled up. Within minutes, though, she was laughing. Her quick recuperation was wondrous to me! She helped me, too–to swing back to reality.

Janeen's suffering was none other than my own. I had already forgiven Charles for murdering my family. But the pain of the trauma had a way of oozing back, or of cracking back sudden as a thunderstorm. Seeing a story on the news, or a film: bang, there it was again. I was back in the bedrooms with Connie, Allen and Bobby, blood everywhere. Yet this short moment with Janeen helped me see how I was being triggered less, how I was healing bit by bit, more and more with each passing day.

When I'm agitated or angry, I have learned that I can refocus my own attention, especially through outdoor mindful walking. However upset, I have learned I can slow down, relax my breathing, take care of my anger.

An excerpt from a letter the year before, the birth year of my first grandchild, the year I vowed to quit smoking, *and did*:

"...We lost three major accounts in our PR business: boom, boom, boom. And how shall we pay the rent? A job suddenly manifested–working for a company that publishes educational materials. I took the bait, thinking, well, perhaps a pension, some dental insurance and a regular paycheck would be in order. I was wrong. I suffered so at the hands of unforgiving business methods that I felt as if someone were walking on my face. I would come home from the job and fall asleep at 7 PM, positively sucked dry.

"On Good Friday, I realized that if I did not do something very soon, I would miss this beautiful spring altogether! So I gave them two weeks notice with a firm conviction never to do such a thing to myself again. I returned to my episodic freelance career, full of renewed gratitude for the way I have made my life. A bit of writing here, a part-time teaching job there, and somehow it all fit together in a pattern where life and work nicely overlap into love. Going into the dungeon of the corporate world every day, I felt utterly cut off from life and light."

In the same letter, I reported my joy at becoming a grandmother: "Watching her face is like watching a windy cloud-strewn sky; she is trying on all the expressions. Her mother Lily was grateful to me for staying about ten days after her birth at their home outside Ft. Lauderdale, FL, to wash, clean and cook while mother and daughter became acquainted in the milky world of the newborn."

Trying to live my adventuresome and often chaotic life, at times, like Janeen, I was trapped in the past of the murders. When one has sustained a deep trauma, the cells of the body remember, and certain triggers can set off the symptoms of shock. Vietnam veteran Claude Anshin Thomas, thirty years after the war and now a Buddhist monk, still sometimes hesitates when reaching for a can of beans from a grocery shelf, thinking, "This can could be booby-trapped." He needs to breathe, calm himself before touching the can. Since the war, he cannot sleep more than two hours straight. For a long time after the murders whenever the phone rang, I felt a stab of fear in my gut and my heart would land in my lap. Or the numbness would begin to set in.

I learned later that the stab of fear is called an *exaggerated startle response*, a symptom from one of the clusters of post-traumatic stress disorder (PTSD) called *hyperarousal*. As in studies that connect post traumatic stress disorder with suicide in men returning from war, after the murders I showed symptoms from all three clusters of PTSD. Besides *hyperarousal* is *avoidance*, or avoiding circumstances that might trigger memories, flashbacks. Most of the family at the time of the murders and still now refuse police reports, newspapers, magazines and conversations about that night. *Avoidance.* This puts another study statistic into perspective—that the family survivors of murder do not begin to deal with their feelings surrounding the murders until an average of ten to twenty years after the event.

The final cluster of PTSD symptoms is *intrusion*: frightening dreams or flashbacks. My own flashback came that night after the murders when I awoke feeling blows on my head. I was certain the blows were coming from a blunt instrument, probably metal. I screamed, waking Philip, who held me. Even though I was not even a blood relative of Connie and the boys, still I suffered from PTSD. Even though the statistics on survivors of homicide do not at all take into account in-laws, aunts, uncles, cousins, neighbors and close friends, this one incident altered my life. How much worse for Connie's mother and sisters and brother, for the grandparents of Allen and Bobby–those tied by blood? How much worse for my own two daughters who adored them.

BATHING THE BABY BUDDHA

From a little spark may burst a flame.

—Dante Alighieri

Our baby Buddha is a bronze color and about one inch long, fashioned of beautifully detailed cast metal. His bed is an incense box with a soft scrap of black velvet as a cover. For our celebration of the Buddha's birth, we brought him out of his bed and invited the children to help us bathe him. For a bathtub, I purchased a bright blue, lotus-shaped dish from Japan. Philip suggested an eye dropper as a ladle to wash the wee statue. To give it a festive look, we tied a gold thread around the eye dropper.

I designed pink flyers to send to the meditation community of Old Path Zendo, now thirty families in all. On each page, I drew a cheerful picture of the baby Buddha with sun and flowers and rain. Since we planned a tea ceremony for the children, we needed to know how many people to expect. So I asked the families to call and reserve a place at the service. Two people responded. One of them would possibly bring a child.

The day arrived. No children came into the meditation hall. We began the Heart Sutra. About halfway through the chanting, my heart beat harder as I heard the small footfalls of little Udae, a six-year-old, flinging open the door and running through the room. We finished the Heart Sutra, and I happily reached for my copy of *Old Path White Clouds*, the life story of the Buddha by Thich Nhat Hanh. Aloud, I read the tale of the baby prince's birth, ending with the story of the visiting sage who tells King Suddhodana, the baby Siddhartha's daddy, "Majesty, you and your country possess great merit to have given birth to such a one as this boy.'"

Then I asked Udae to share with us a story, or a stretch, or a song. He gave us the song of "Who Built the Ark? Noah, Noah" from his summer Bible school. I passed out shiny, tumbled pebbles and suggested a pebble meditation, breathing and smiling with the bell. At our seats, with each complete breath, we picked up a pebble and moved it from left to right; when they are all moved to the right, we moved them back from right to left. We completed about ten breaths. I notice the Moss Garden incense was fragrant as earth herself.

There were six of us in all. We lined up to bathe the tiny statue of the child, and after each washing with the eye-dropper, we made a lotus blossom of our hands and bowed in a heartfelt way to the baby. My tears of joy helped water the child.

I passed the teacups and cloth napkins. Then we slid a tray of rice crackers, strawberries and Swiss chocolate and a teapot of apricot nectar, from person to person. We accepted each offering with our hands in a lotus blossom, bowing. Every gesture had meaning and depth. With mindfulness, each moment shone like a jewel—the sound of the nectar filling the cup, the scent of the chocolate, the whoosh of the tea tray sliding across the wooden floor.

At the end I asked Udae to dry the baby prince and put him back into his bed. With great care, Udae patted the little Buddha dry with a clean napkin and placed him in the incense box. Udae arranged the velvet cover so the baby's tiny face was showing—that he might breathe.

By the following February, we were almost homeless. "It is a mistake to believe that one has a fixed home." I had no sooner penned these words to begin an essay on impermanence than the telephone broke the silence. It was our landlord to inform us that she would be raising the rent by two thirds. I received the news quietly and told her we will probably have to leave. She was silent.

Nineteen years we had lived there with a fixed low rent, thanks to her patronage: I knew the rooms by heart. Two of our dogs, two cats and a gerbil were buried in the back yard. The compost heap was seasoned; the earth expected it. The garlic was about to sprout in the herb garden I built with a circle of fieldstones. The iris waited. It had been an unseasonably warm winter. Although it was February, the snowdrops and aconite covered the ground with their delicate whites and jolly yellows. In the time we had been there, they had quintupled in number.

Outrageous! A friend tells me. She cannot do this to you! Withhold your rent! Get a lawyer! Picket her house! But I did not want to poison my system with anger. I had been glad to honor the old manor house and to have raised my children there—my children who were by then raising children of their own. We were grateful to have seen so many seasons come and go on this old holdout farm in a region where the farm fields were being deeply gouged with the machines of construction, where million-dollar houses and billion-dollar shopping centers were sprouting to blacktop the land.

In the zendo, I lit a candle, chanted the heart sutra, prostrated myself, taking refuge. I stopped thinking for a while.

A zendo is a beautifully portable room. Humans, with our rainproof skin, our working legs and willing hands, are beautifully portable, too. Indeed, our brains are ideally designed for challenge. I felt challenged, and I was willing to go. It would be a mistake, after all, to believe that one has a fixed home.

JAIL CELL, MONK'S CELL

"Minds innocent and quiet take [prison] ...for a hermitage,"

–John Lovelace

Bending to enter the conference room where we held meditation at Countytown Prison in Pennsylvania, Joshua darkened the doorway. He did not stand; he loomed. Joshua was a scary-looking six-foot-three or four, over three hundred pounds, with a blue anarchist tattoo inked into his shaved scalp. It was a Thursday evening in the second year of our weekly visits to Countytown. A Zen master's warning flashed in my mind: "Don't leave a drunk or a bum outside the monastery gate; you might be excluding the Lord Buddha."

We did not ask about Joshua's jail time. Not long after he began his prison sentence, the doctors had diagnosed him with schizophrenia and placed him on antipsychotic drugs. Perhaps because of the heavy drug dosages, he was a mouth breather, adding to his sinister aura.

Back at Countytown, hugging practice, with three slow breaths, invented by Thich Nhat Hanh as a way to be truly present with one another, became a ritual. Since inmates are ordinarily denied the luxury of human touch, I wondered how many of them attended meditation just for the motherly, fatherly hugs that Philip and I enjoyed with each of them before saying goodbye each week. We practiced hugging meditation to be truly present to each other through three complete shared breaths. Afterwards, we bowed with our palms joined in a lotus bud. It was not we who initiated the hugging, either. It was the men, these streetwise youngsters whose personalities morphed the moment they walked out the door of the conference room and returned to the prison halls—their street. Out would pop the exaggerated swagger of boys who had not been properly fathered, the street jive. Thus I began to look deeply at some of the peer pressures on these men. As I got to know them as real and vulnerable and in certain ways, innocent, my fears abated. There is no self and other.

After many months at Countytown, four inmates were growing solid in their meditation and mindfulness practice. Big Joshua was one of them. Over the months that Joshua attended weekly meditation, my fears gave way to his enthusiasm. I watched with utter happiness as he took to the practice like an eagle to air, making of his jail cell a monk's cell. He asked profound questions, ordered books on Buddhism and read them cover to cover, recited the Four Noble Truths and the Heart Sutra, studied the five *skandhas*–form, feelings, perceptions, mental formations (or habit patterns) and consciousness. Josh was a wide-mouthed jar, filling, filling.

"I ordered books from Thich Nhat Hanh's Parallax Press, Zen Mountain Monastery, Richard Gere's Foundation, and from Bo and Sita Lozoff of the Human Kindness Foundation and the Prison Ashram Project," Josh boldly told us at the prison. "The meditation practice makes me look forward to every day," he said, "Breathing in and breathing out, working on my form and lack of form. I've found a way to discipline myself, a way to counter the chaos."

Josh's typical prison day began at 4:30 or 5 AM, when he sat in meditation for forty-five minutes and practiced walking meditation like a cat, pacing the limited confines of his cell. Then he chanted sutras. At 8, he went to work in the commissary warehouse, a coveted minimum-security-status job that Joshua attained only after three years of good behavior, accomplished through his knack for mindfulness. After work and dinner in the prison cafeteria, he routinely sat in meditation again for fifteen to twenty minutes. Then he would read from his growing Buddhist library and go to bed.

But it had not always been a monk's cell and minimum security for Joshua. "I started out my prison time right away getting into trouble for fighting. There was this new guy on the block. He must've figured you start with the biggest man and work your way down, because he first picked a fight with me. So I just lifted him up with one hand and split his temple with the other. For that I got twenty-eight days in the hole."

"What's the hole?"

"Well, it's a four-by-nine-foot cell that holds a bed, a desk, a toilet, and a sink. The guards take you out every other day for a shower. You have contact with guards only. The officers were actually pretty cool with me."

"What would you do if that inmate picked a fight with you today?" I asked him.

"Nothing," Joshua quietly replied.

Thich Nhat Hanh addresses anger in a book he wrote for inmates, *Be Free Where You Are*. He tells the story of the bombing of Ben Tre, the home town of his close colleague, Sister Chan Khong, during the US/Vietnam War. Because there were five or six guerrillas there, one officer claimed he had to bomb and destroy the town and its inhabitants to save the country from communism. Thay was very angry. But he knew already that the energy of anger creates trouble wherever it arises. So he developed the habit of using poetry as therapy, just as I have always done. After the bombs, after the killing, he wrote a famous poem about holding his own face in his two hands to keep his soul from flying out in anger. As a monk, he had already learned to care for his anger as if it were a crying baby. Joshua had no such training. Nor did Charles, the murderer. A monk learns not to act on his anger, but to take care of it, to hold his face gently in his own two hands, thus allowing joy and happiness to return.

About a year after Philip and I bequeathed the prison sangha to Steven and moved to North Carolina to found Cloud Cottage Sangha, Joshua phoned us to say he was out of jail. We had stayed in touch, and now he had an important request.

"I want to receive the Five Mindfulness Trainings," he said, indicating his interest in entering the stream of our practice tradition.

"We're hosting a dharma teacher from California, Lyn Fine, in North Carolina this September, Josh," I said. "If you can get yourself here you can stay with us, and we can arrange a ceremony to have Lyn and the sangha offer you the precepts." Offering the precepts meant that Lyn would transmit to Josh and others in a formal ceremony the Five Trainings that Philip and I received from Lyn at Old Path Zendo.

It took a huge effort on Joshua's part to make the journey from Pennsylvania to North Carolina. First he secured permission from his halfway house to go on leave for religious reasons. Then he got the okay from his supervisor to take a leave of absence from his job. Finally, he needed money for bus fare. His grandmother complied with a loan. We set a date for his arrival.

On the long Greyhound ride, Joshua wrote untitled poems:

Impermanence is the
only constant.
Change is the one true
quality.
Suffering, joy, hate,
love, these too
shall pass. Sitting still
I center,
Quiet my mind,
Rest in the joy of
my breath.

Josh's bus arrived on time. Back at Cloud Cottage, which is truly a cottage in size, Lyn slept on the futon in the den and Joshua put his giant body down on our living room couch.

"I have to talk to you," he said. "I have a question. Can someone who's a sex offender receive the precepts? I...I'm not sure I can do this because of my crime. And Judith, I don't even remember what I did! I was blacked out on drugs!"

Ironically, just at that moment into our back door came a sangha member who had been repeatedly sexually abused as a child. Just as she walked in, bearing a gift of soup, I was answering Joshua, "Of course you can receive the Trainings. Your past doesn't matter." My mind raced in quick succession to: Charles Grand raping my sister-in-law and murdering her: the Buddha accepting the penitent mass murderer, Angulimala, as one of his monks: Jesus taking supper with prostitutes.

Fortunately, our friend with the soup at the back door escaped hearing any of this conversation, or it might have made her dinner difficult. Just then, Lyn Fine came out of the other room to join us, and I introduced her to my friend. We served my friend's carrot soup with a hearty bread. There we were, an unlikely gathering, teachers, perpetrators, victims—no self, no other—gathered for a mindful meal, a true Zen Eucharist. In this way, we practiced interbeing.

Lyn led the retreat that weekend, in Lee and Alice Johnson's screen house set on a vast, tree-dotted lawn in a mountain cove. On a crystal autumn day of marigolds and maple leaves, we held the ceremony for the transmission of the Five Mindfulness Trainings. Tearfully, I watched as Joshua brought his massive body down to touch the earth, receiving each of the Three Refuges:

I take refuge in the Buddha,
one who shows me the way in this life;
I take refuge in the Sangha,
the community that lives in harmony and awareness;
I take refuge in the Dharma,
the way of understanding and love.

As I watched Josh prostrate his enormous bulk, bringing his knees and forehead to touch the earth, his palms upraised, a piece of me was liberated. My guilt and regret at never having contacted Charles Grand to say in person, "I forgive you," was gone. My Dharma journey from murder to forgiveness had come full circle in this moment. "I forgive you, Judith," I whispered to myself.

After the ceremony, Lyn gave Joshua his lineage name, Peaceful Light of the Source, linking it to mine and Philip's, also given to us by her—Clear Light of the Source and Flowing Stream of the Source. I was able to see on his ordination day that Joshua's journey was my journey. Joshua and I inter-exist. Despite a long and bumpy ride, I, too, was learning to "rest in the joy of the breath." Like Josh, I was unfolding my heart to the perfect understanding that transforms hatred and degradation into love and forgiveness.

In the chaos of prison life, Josh had longed for peace. There, he had come to discover his inner teacher, his true self. Back home in Pennsylvania, after the ceremony, he founded Dharma Rain Sangha.

"I met one of the Countytown guards on the outside who told me, 'I knew you didn't belong in there,'" he said. But maybe he did belong in there. How else for this gentle giant? How else would Joshua's Dharma journey have begun?

My friendship with Josh led to publication of his story in the international quarterly for English speaking students of Thich Nhat Hanh, which led to correspondence with other inmates. The correspondence project between Old Path Sangha and Serene Lotus Petal Sangha flourished. Some of our letters were eventually published in a Princeton, New Jersey holistic health magazine. This led to more individual correspondences with inmates who practice Buddhism behind bars.

Locked up, at times in solitary confinement, these men are face to face with their forgiveness issues every day. Here is one of the most revealing and transformative letters I ever received from an inmate, whom I call Z. Printed with his permission, this letter is included here because the author (not Joshua) felt intuitively his words could help someone, someday. Here from a sex offender in one of North Carolina's prisons in March, 2007, is perhaps the deepest, most poignant insight into the mind of the murderer of my family. All three men—Joshua, Charles and Z, whose letter is below–committed sex crimes (and in Charles case, mass murder) for which they should and did pay. The difference here is that Joshua's crime was committed in a drug-induced blackout, while this man's crime, as well as the murders of my family, was planned and executed in cold blood. I include it because this letter demonstrates that contrition is possible—that a person can take full responsibility for his crime and the suffering he caused, and can be rehabilitated. The Buddha thought so, too. Do I trust that Z will not repeat his crime? I have no way of knowing. But as long as he is able to maintain the state of mind of this letter through mindfulness practice and therapy, I believe he will not rape again. First, his letter to me. Then his letter to his victim.

Affixed at the top of the page with cellophane tape are four tiny, delicate flowers, once colorful, now browned with age, with a handwritten label— from "H" yard, M. Correctional.

Dear Judith,

I am so glad you had a good retreat. I felt enriched by your description. What a gift it is to have traveled there with you.

Impermanence! My own retreat to segregation was short lived. I ended up in a discipline hearing and the charges were dropped. My supervisor at SOAR [Survivors of Abuse in Recovery, Inc.] *put in a good word for me so they cut me a break and I kept my job. I spent my time in the hole productively. I did some yoga poses I usually don't get a chance to do. So imagine a 5x7 cell with a toilet and sink combo unit, a steel bunk and an inmate standing on his head! All in all it was a valuable lesson. I learned about myself and about being mindful.*

I got the <u>Right View Quarterly</u> you sent (Thank you!). And one of the first articles I read really made me *think–James Hickling's "Unhitching the Cart." The part that struck me is when he talked about forgiving himself for the pain he caused <u>himself</u> and all the karma <u>he has yet to experience</u> because of his actions. I realized that I still have negative karma that I set in motion long ago. I feel I can mindfully experience it with equanimity and transmute it into positive ends instead of reacting to it and creating more karma. That's a beautiful step!*

So I'm out of the hole and it was a beautiful day today. Yesterday, I was walking the yard and noticed a patch of clover growing voraciously. It was thick and dark green and inviting me to sit. So I sat. A small pleasure.

I enjoyed your article in RVQ too. I especially like Derek Lin's Taoist story [See p. 223] at the end. I'm using it to help one of my participants who has a lot of resentment toward his father. His crime was a need for power and control and revenge toward a father who he believed stole that from him. One insight I had into the story is that I cannot just drop the potatoes of my resentments and pretend they don't exist. I have to understand the potatoes/resentments in relation to myself and realize it is "me/my bag" holding it. But if I never look at the rotten potatoes or the bag, I never even think to drop the bag. I just pretend it doesn't exist and wonder why my back hurts and everything smells bad. The best I can do is forgive, because that person was just acting out their own suffering. I can choose to end the cycle of anger through forgiveness, by looking into my anger and transcending my own narrow view of it through my illusionary self.

I was inspired to write a letter. I'm not exactly sure why, but I just felt it was the right thing to do. I was thinking about the ladies you see in prison, [note: at that time I was teaching mindfulness in a women's prison] *and about your Dharma friend who was abused as a child. We do an exercise in here called a Clarification Letter, where we tell the truth to our victims in a letter. I had the notion that someday you might come upon a person who could use this letter. I'm working on faith here. I am not asking you to give it to anyone. I just get the impression that someday someone will ask for it or it will be apparent whom to give it to. Does that sound crazy? I normally don't do things like this, but it was just clear to me that this was what I was supposed to do next. Anyway, feel free to do with it what you see fit. Perhaps I just needed to re-write it for me? (See below.)*

Thank you for all the quotes. I love to collect quotes in my journal. One of my favorites: "Really good people make you feel like you too can become great."—Mark Twain

The days to my release keep getting shorter and shorter. July 22 is fast approaching. It's hard not to think about it, looming on the horizon like a full moon. I'm both excited and nervous. I found out about the Deep River Sangha in Greensboro, where I am going. They meet on Sundays. I'm looking forward to being able to practice on the outside and hopefully make some new friends. I'm planning on going back to college to finish my degree. I'm thinking either social work or psychology.

Thank you so much for your friendship. It means so much to me. I hope you continue to have joyful days. I bow to the Buddha in you.

Fondly,
Z.

To My Victim:
You do not have to read this letter if you do not want to. It is completely your choice whether to continue or not.

I will not pretend to know all you are going through. The pain, confusion, frustration, shame, guilt and anger must feel overwhelming at times. I want to tell you that the abuse was not your fault. It was all my fault. I tricked you into doing it by pretending it was okay and pretending to be nice, kind and loving. I pretended we were playing a game. I forced you to go along with what I wanted because I was bigger and physically stronger than you were. I'd yell and scream a lot and be mean sometimes so you would be afraid of me—so you would be too scared to say no. Then, after the abuse, I would pretend that everything was normal. My being these two very different people must have been confusing to you.

I told you lies. Lots of lies. I told you I loved you, but my actions said otherwise. I took advantage of you because you were younger, and innocent. You were a child and you trusted grownups; and I violated that trust. I can only imagine how hard it must be for you to trust others now. I took such a good quality in you and used it against you, which is a horrible thing to do to another human being.

I knew what I was doing was wrong, and I knew you did not want me to do it, but at that time I did not care about you or your feelings. I was completely selfish and cared only about what I wanted. I treated you like an object and not the person you are. I know you probably went along with me and did what I wanted because you were scared, and not because you wanted it or liked it.

I chose you as my victim because you were there. You just happened to be in the line of fire because you were my step-daughter. I directed all my inner anger and rage onto you because I was too weak and ignorant to confront my own demons. I lacked the self-awareness and courage to ask for help. I felt weak and powerless, and you were innocent and full of life and joy. I saw in you everything I felt I lacked and it made me so jealous. I took all my anger out on you. In my wrong and distorted thinking I thought if I hurt you it would make me feel better. I thought I would have revenge on all the people and on an unfair world I was so mad at. I wrongly thought the power and control I could have over you by hurting you would make me feel strong. Of course it doesn't ever work that way. I was filled with more shame, self-hatred and anger and likely dumped all that same garbage onto you.

People often want to know if I will offend again. I have been through over 600 hours of sex offender treatment and have spent four years in prison working on changing my offending behavior. I have learned that other people are human beings and have feelings just like me. Nobody deserves to be treated like I treated you. I feel very sorry for all the pain I caused you and your family and friends. I think about how much I changed your life through my selfish actions and I truly do not ever again want to cause anyone the harm I caused you. My goal is NO MORE VICTIMS. I have come to know that I can be mindful and responsible and take care of my anger, suffering and stress without taking it out on others.

A sex offense is never okay. No one deserves it. No one asks for it. There is no excuse. I wrote this letter because I think you deserve the truth, as ugly as it is, and to clarify the lies I told you.

I hope in some small way this helps you find your inner power to continue courageously on your journey. May you be free and find your true home.

Sincerely,
A Sex Offender

INSIDE THE BURNING

A mystic sits inside the burning. There are wonderful shapes in rising smoke that imagination loves to watch. But it's a mistake to leave the fire for that filmy sight. Stay here at the flame's core.

—Rumi

The first retreat held at Rolling Green Farm took place in the Fall of 1998, a year after my ordination by Thich Nhat Hanh into the lay branch of the Order of Interbeing. By then we had removed the office furniture, made the mantle and hearth into an altar, and Genro had formally dedicated the room as Old Path Zendo. On each of three days, we were scheduled for one-on-one interviews with Genro, during which he would encourage us in the practice of remaining still and silent for hours on end.

As I began to sit for long hours that weekend, nothing happened. Not uncommon. I was cook, too, for this retreat. I prepared some of the food a full day ahead of the weekend, and exited the meditation hall about an hour before each meal to assemble, heat, bake, set the tables and create a buffet. So my thoughts were consumed with the care and feeding of a dozen people. That made it easy to be distracted from the focus necessary for meditation.

But in the oven of *zazen*, as my mind and heart baked, I began to feel strongly the suffering of others. I had already cracked the barrier of my own suffering at that first retreat and subsequent others. Once again, I sat on my cushion with tears coursing down my cheeks, praying not to disturb the other sitters. Specifically, I felt the suffering of Connie and Allen and Bobby, of the boy who murdered them, and the anguish of my family.

Also I felt the suffering of the people of Nicaragua, at that time, in the wake of a harrowing earthquake there. And that of my dad who was dying back in Cleveland, Ohio. Compassion had arisen in me: I embodied their suffering.

It was the moment for my dharma interview with the teacher. I entered the breakfast room where we had set up a miniature altar and two cushions. A delicate, inviting incense was burning. Pure peace. I bowed, stepped to my cushion, bowed again, seated myself facing Genro's imposing Zen self in black robes, and bowed a third time, as is protocol. I spoke to him of my deep concern, the pain I was feeling. He advised me to avoid getting trapped in the suffering, to go beneath it. I remembered his former advice to "stay with the suffering." Now he was telling me to move on!

"Sometimes it helps to dedicate your suffering to a specific person," he said. No contest. I would dedicate my suffering-for-others to my father who had been diagnosed with congestive heart failure.

Back on my cushion I was able to dive to the bottom of my affliction, breaking through its crust. I imagined dying to be like this. I came to a very still place, like a cave. There I felt mind and body as one. Not *my* mind and body, but Big Mind, Big Body. Solid as stone.

During each sitting period of thirty-five to forty minutes, because we stood to practice walking meditation between sittings, I found I had to repeat the process interrupted by the walking, to dive through the crust of suffering in order to return to the still-as-a-stone stage. This was the second day, and Genro urged me on, to push even deeper.

"Use your peace," he said.

We were practicing noble silence, even at meals. Meditation ended promptly at 9 PM, when we went to bed without any distractions. Sleep became my meditation, dreamless and sweet.

By Sunday I had become adept at breath-surfing to the still-as-a-stone cave where my heart, so big and juicy during the anguish was now insignificant as a crumb. And as I traveled deeper to the bottom of the well within, there opened a light beyond tenderness. This was God light, Big Mind—warm and sufficient and safe, composed of total harmony. This was light beyond light. I had gone beyond logic to love, a love that knew no bounds.

Throughout the journey, I held my father in the palm of my hand. Even as a great peace flowered in me, I longed to bring back to him and others this message: *complete peace is available to all of us, with no exceptions, all the time.*

FLAME TO FLAME

A glimmering, maybe a knowing like soft, red warm glowing
of coals in a late night campfire.

– Stuart Heady, from the poem "Galisteo Campfire"

We give to the living what we owe to the dead. Years after the abortion, I was handed an opportunity to forgive myself once and for all.

Carole showed up in our lives about the time Philip and I were married in 1981. She had just been diagnosed with PKD—Polycystic Kidney Disease–the disease her father died of when she was fifteen. Carole was in love. She had moved in with our friend the late Robert DeVoe, quirky artist, theosophist and intellectual, into a town house in Lambertville, New Jersey on the Delaware River. DeVoe, as he was known, strung some ceramic beads and presented them to Carole as worry beads. She went nowhere without them. When we met, I had just walked out of the shower with a towel on my head, and Carole says she fell in love with me. I say time folded in that instant, and without words or images getting in the way, she knew that part of me would literally someday become part of her.

Carole's life was like a night watch on the hell shift. In May of 2000, her kidneys stopped functioning altogether. The surgery to remove both of her football-sized organs riddled with cysts nearly killed her. The doctors surgically placed a shunt in her arm and Carole began the depressing, laborious life of one on hemodialysis. The site of the shunt became infected and the pain was almost unbearable. Her emotions were tumultuous, a slippery slope, headed downwards.

"For me," she said, "dialysis was a form of dying. Then when they took my kidneys out, my fluid intake was severely limited. I remember looking at orange soda, which I never liked, and coveting it. And if you drank too much, the next dialysis session was even more painful. I did not assume the transplant was going to happen until it happened."

In February of 2000, Carole sent me a desperate email asking for a mantra, a prayer, anything to help her. I gave her the idea of dedicating her pain to another person or group of persons, as I had read people in the hospital often did for Mother Teresa. In a photo of the famous sculpture of "The Three Servicemen" at the Vietnam Veterans Memorial in Washington, D.C., Carole saw the eyes of grief, of stoicism, of all the suffering the three men had seen. "If they could do that, I can do this," she reasoned. She decided to dedicate her pain to the US/Vietnam War veterans, and in this way, still turning away when they put the needles in, she barely survived the pain and degradation that was dialysis.

In March, 2000, I picked up the telephone and dialed Carole's number. She answered with a weary hello. For the twenty years I had known her, Carole had always been a vibrant woman who would break into song at the least provocation, mostly Broadway tunes, changing the words to suit the moment—a talented social worker—a generous lover of life. She had chosen to remain childless because she did not want to pass on faulty genes. Her brother, Marc's kidneys were failing as we spoke.

"I want to get tested to give you my kidney," I told her.

"Well, first of all, the chances are slim that we'll be a match," she said. Carole was deathly sick and depressed again.

"I have a feeling," I said.

"I don't want to get my hopes up again," she countered. Carol had received well-meaning offers of help that had faded to nothing.

"At least find out if you can receive the kidney of someone with Rh-negative factor in their blood."

"Jude, are you thinking this through?"

"Yes, I'm sure. I'll call my doctor."

The answer came back yes. That was the first in a series of yeses that ultimately led to the surgery. But I knew. I knew from the first phone call—no, from my first inner inkling—that I would give Carole my kidney. And I am not at all prescient. The first blood tests were thrown out by the University of Pennsylvania Hospital because we did not label the vials according to their instructions. The second batch, looking for blood antigen matches, came back good, two out of six possible matches. When I first saw my friend at home in Princeton when she was on dialysis, I hardly recognized her as my Carole. She looked more like an Auschwitz victim—skeletal, eyes huge and drawn by dark circles, her complexion sallow as death. She could barely walk.

What a comedy of errors, getting to the series of tests in Philadelphia at the University of Pennsylvania Hospital. I stayed in a quaint downtown B&B with another dear friend who was doing research at the University of Pennsylvania Archeological Museum. She snored and kept me up all night. The luxurious Jacuzzi feature on the bathtub malfunctioned and flooded the bathroom. On our way to the testing site, we got hopelessly mired and lost in the Philadelphia rush hour. But the test results were good. Even the stone-faced transplant coordinator hugged me, tearing up, because the head nephrologist had just told us the surgery was all but certain. When I arrived at Carole's house in Princeton that night, she was out at the dialysis unit. I entered the den and approached Lorin, her husband, who was reading his paper.

"Lorin, the surgeons tell me it looks like a go." He grabbed me and his glasses fell off and the newspaper crunched between us as we hugged and cried. The next morning, when the final tests came through positive, Carole and I had a similar scene, our hearts full to bursting with gratitude.

The icing on the cake was that doctors confirmed I was a candidate to undergo the less intrusive laparoscopic surgery for removal of my kidney.

In the meantime, birthdays and death days and real estate trading continued apace. In Cleveland, my father was still dying at home of congestive heart failure, and after renting for over a year, Philip and I were in the process of purchasing our first tiny house, Cloud Cottage, in Black Mountain. On summer leave from my teaching job at a charming private school, I planned to go back to work soon after surgery. My mother poured out her support for my decision, even though she was in the midst of the struggle to single-handedly care for my father in his last days. Hospice had been called in. Daddy did not want me to do the surgery. "What if your remaining kidney fails?" he asked. We never told him about the surgery.

Our kidneys exist to ensure we're not poisoned by an accumulation of our own waste. While the daily flow of blood through the kidneys is about 425 gallons, a mere thousandth of this is converted to urine. Each kidney is composed of a million or so nephrons, or filters which, if unwound and placed end to end, would stretch for more than fifty miles. I drew a cartoon of my left kidney, the gift kidney, with a face and a gloved, waving hand, and in the voice bubble: "Here Ah* come, Carole!" The asterisked note read, "Jude's kidney has quickly assimilated into the South."

The procedure itself was a jewel on a chain of sparkling and profound events. I remember taking the long walk to the transplant unit, down what seemed like blocks of narrow corridors at the U of P Hospital with Lorin and Carole's mother, Claire, and Carole in a wheelchair. Mentally, I recited a prayer from my teacher, Thich Nhat Hanh: *I have arrived, I am home in the here and the now; I am solid, I am free; I am solid, I am free; in the ultimate I dwell; in the ultimate I dwell.*

At the desk where we signed in, Carole almost fainted. We were assigned to separate rooms–"Just in case something goes wrong"–so Carole and I talked on the phone.

"The night before the surgery," said Carole, "the team did a last-minute compatibility test. Out of anxiety, I curled into a fetal position. I wouldn't believe it was truly happening until they wheeled me into the O. R. In the meantime, Jude slept peacefully, assured that everything would be fine."

My dear and supportive Philip, now working for the American Red Cross, was absent by my request. Our two faithful, adoring daughters, Lily and Rachel had arrived from the South, each with a toddler in tow, so there was a familial air of celebration in the room. But beneath the festivity was tension, their unasked question: What if this doesn't work? Carole's doubts. I had prepared myself like a vestal virgin using my doctor's herbal kidney tonic, through diet and exercise, through prayers and affirmations, and through—okay, this may sound farfetched but it worked—talking to my kidneys and saying thank you. My doctor and friend Sal D'Angio, integrative physician, treated me pre- and post-surgery *pro bono*.

The morning of the big event, my daughters administered the herbals and homeopathies prescribed by Sal. There was one complication: once they got inside, the surgeons discovered an extra artery attached to my left kidney. So for me, the surgery was longer than expected, six hours. In the meantime, the transplant team had prepped Carole in the adjoining O. R. The moment the surgeon, Dr. Markmann, placed my kidney in Carole's waiting open abdomen, it began secreting urine.

"I feel alert," Carole told the doctors. And they were jubilant. They were thrilled with the urine output of her new kidney. "I was in a state of shock—terrified, to tell the truth," she said. "Some people have to stay on dialysis for a while after a transplant. Some kidneys don't work. I remember Jude walking into my room the next day—the loving looks we gave each other." This was the moment of recognition that we truly inter-are. Carole now had a chance to be alive and free, no longer attached to a machine.

Both of us have thrived ever since. And I have learned to thank my body parts often and thoroughly. While rejection episodes are the norm for transplant patients, Carole has defied the statistics. To date, many years later, she has not had a single such episode. The nurses were surprised when I refused their offers of morphine. All I needed was Extra-Strength Tylenol. Carole's recovery was painful, long and slow. But now we were blood sisters. Truly, there is no self and other.

It was not until much later that through the miracle of this exchange of organs with my friend, I felt I had cleansed the negative karma of my abortion, or that the scales were somehow in balance again. Not that it is right to kill and to give a life in return. Even though I did not give my kidney for this reason, I know now there are things we can do to right the wrongs we have done. I once heard Thich

Nhat Hanh advise a long-suffering Vietnam veteran who had killed many children to find the starving children of the world in the here and now, and to help them. With the gift of my kidney, my karma was cleansed, I felt absolved, and my life could unfold in beauty.

SITTING ON FIRE

...Practice like fire. Whether you throw into fire cloth or paper or flowers or dirty things, the fire accepts all and burns all. Whether it is fragrant or whether it stinks, the fire accepts all and the fire reduces everything to ash and smoke, because fire has the power to transform....

— Buddha, from *Old Path White Clouds,*
by Thich Nhat Hanh

Thirteen years had elapsed since I had first heard about *Village des Pruniers*, Plum Village. In the meantime, I had become Thay's student and was ordained. This was my first visit to my teacher's home monastery.

When my kidney sister Carole offered me the trip to Plum Village as a way of saying thank you for her new life, I recruited Lucy as my traveling companion. What a marvelous experience, I thought, for a twelve-year-old: Plum Village, where children are treated as the special guests they truly are, lovingly spoiled by monks and nuns who would likely not have children of their own, but would compensate with these young spiritual descendents. After a week in Paris, we traveled to Plum Village for the Summer Opening, a six-week practice period for lay students and families to live at the monastery. Plum Village consists of several hamlets, some separated by as much as a half-hour's walk. In each of the hamlets is a large meditation hall and at least one lotus pond with lotuses descended from Vietnam. In Plum Village, Lucy and I walked painterly paths over hills hugged by grape arbors as far as the eye could see, bordering endless splashes of sunflower fields in full bloom. The green rolling landscape was punctuated with the red tile roofs of country cottages and barns. A large troop of children, thoroughly indulged by the monastics in charge, climbed pine trees to collect their nuts and squirrel them away for snacks, and tumbled through meadows, playing basketball with the monks.

Lucy stockpiled pine nuts on a shelf which normally served as an altar in our room in a several-hundred-year-old stone building. Nearby in the Upper Hamlet was a stone wall where a fierce battle had taken place during World War II. Thay tells us it took about 20 years to transform the dark war energy along that wall to the energy of peace and joy. Now in a niche of the wall stands a small statue of *Avalokitesvara*, or *Quan Yin*, the bodhisattva of compassion—she who hears the cries of the world—where monastics and visitors offer incense and flowers.

It was Hiroshima Day, 2001, thirteen years after the murders. I still had bouts of emotional turmoil. We stayed in the Upper Hamlet where generous monks lived in tents so they could offer their rooms to retreatants. We were each assigned a small family group led by a monk and a lay practitioner. How gentle this family group compared to the family group of the alcohol rehab who screamed at me those long years ago back in Pennsylvania. During a tearful discussion with my group in the bamboo grove, I told my true nightmare of that night, three of my family murdered. I told of how I had come to meet our teacher shortly thereafter, and of how I had learned to embrace my grief and pain–how unexpectedly, after five years of stilling my mind daily, that suddenly, spontaneously, I forgave the boy who did it. How after that, Philip and I began taking our mindfulness practice to a prison where some of the men had known the murderer, who by then had hung himself to death in his jail cell. How I regret that I never told the boy "I forgive you."

The pace at Plum Village is slower than the Deep South in summer. On "lazy days" we took the whole day to wash our clothes by hand and hang them on the line near giant sunflowers, sentinels of the vegetable garden. Together with our multilingual family group, we chopped vegetables in afternoons, according to instructions, vegetables to be transformed by monk chefs into delectable veggie fare. I had never known there were so many ways to prepare tofu! At night, although our teacher did not join us, there were festivals incorporating music, puppet skits, plays, drumming circles and dance.

Everywhere, all day long, where we walked, there was music. I had packed my Native American flute made in Black Mountain of local river cane. When

I lent it out and heard it played by Jeff Smith of Belgium–I swear like Pan in the forest of *A Midsummer Night's Dream*–I told him to keep the instrument for himself. One often heard simple and childlike tunes, especially this one that has become the theme song of Plum Village. "Breathing In, Breathing Out" entered the hearts of those of us who were there that summer:

Breathing in, breathing out
Breathing in, breathing out
I am blooming as a flower; I am fresh as the dew.
I am solid as a mountain; I am firm as the earth.
I am free.

Breathing in, breathing out
Breathing in, breathing out
I am water reflecting what is real, what is true
And I feel there is space deep inside of me.
I am free, I am free, I am free.

Mornings belonged to Thay. About 10, he would offer a generous dharma talk in one or another of the hamlets. Routinely there would be a morning meditation, a mindful breakfast, the pilgrimage on foot to the designated hamlet, all in silence. We would leave our hundreds of pairs of shoes and sandals outside the door and enter the meditation hall with a bow. The altar flowers were always a surprise– accomplished with sticks and grasses and unexpected elements, free of cliché, taken from Plum Village gardens and arranged by monks and lay visitors. On entering the huge hall, Lucy and I had the tasks of finding a place to sit (Is there room up front?), locating a pair of earphones and plugging them into one of the media stations for translations into English.

Then the subdued excitement of waiting for Thay to arrive in the dharma hall. As he finally did arrive, there would be the shuffle and hush of several hundred people, as we all stood in reverence with palms joined. All this without voices, only the padding of stockinged feet, brush of clothing, plump of pillows, clearing of throats. Then the chanting of monks and nuns, the bells, the drums. Thay would teach in one of three languages–French, English or Vietnamese. With 30 or so languages represented that summer, sitting in the dharma hall was like sitting in the assembly of the United Nations.

After whispered translations of some of the deepest teachings I had ever heard, we would walk with Thay for an hour or so, the children surrounding him as I imagine Jesus walked in Judea. Hundreds of us went softly, not as single drops but as a flowing stream, up hill and down, alongside brooks, through the plum orchards that gave the place its name, uphill to see far over the undulating countryside, downhill through well-packed paths in the forest. Every leaf, every flower shone. Our feet touched the earth with such a deep and silent peace that the leaves of grass must have laughed for joy.

Thay held my granddaughter's hand during the long walk one morning. I asked Lucy later, "How did it feel to hold Thay's hand?" There was a group gathered around us.

"Moomah," she said, using her pet name for me, "It was just a hand!" A friend offered, "That's the very reason Thay keeps the children around him."

On another occasion, I, too, had a chance to hold Thay's hand. It happened a few years later when a group of us—a hundred or so– who had practiced walking meditation that morning, sat down with our teacher in a circle of stones in a live oak grove at the Deer Park Monastery in California. All eyes were on Thay. The tiny Vietnamese girl in a brown monk's suit whose hand he had held during the walk, sat closely next to him. Then Thay offered us a photo op, as one by one we sat beside him and had our pictures snapped. When friends literally pushed me into the inner circle to sit beside him, I leaned over to him and whispered, "Dear Thay, I hold your hand with me wherever I go." At which point he took my hand.

And I can tell you it was not just a hand–it was the wing of a butterfly.

The children and I, that summer of 2001 at Plum Village, composed a puppet play, "The Wedding of the Sun and Moon," for a performance at the Full Moon Festival at the edge of the lotus pond in Upper Hamlet. We built giant parade-style puppets from scrounged plywood and mounted them on thick, lightweight bamboo poles. Then we surrounded them with generous amounts of fabric that flew in the breeze. The night of the performance, a flutist from the Vienna Symphony Orchestra magically appeared to lead us like a piper. About fifty of us in line snaked out from the children's hut across the meadow to the lotus pond with our giant sun and giant moon, their huge cardboard hands outstretched. Maybe twenty-five star-shaped puppets hung from shorter bamboo poles carried by dozens of kids. Our culminating song was "'Tis a Gift to be Simple, 'Tis a Gift to be Free." At that moment, I felt it–simple and free.

Brandon, the lay practitioner co-leading our group, asked if I would tell my forgiveness story to the gathered community that night at the Hiroshima Commemoration ceremony. He asked if I would explain how the event of the murders stemmed from the roots of violence in our culture. I took a deep breath and agreed. So Hiroshima Day, 2001, became the seed of this book. I thank Brandon for suggesting I tell my story, as the telling and re-telling has helped me heal.

What I did not realize at the time was that my daughter Lily had never had occasion to tell *her* daughter, my granddaughter, this story. Lucy had been a baby at the time of the murders, and Lily had never found the right hour or venue. How do you introduce a child to this level of horror?

The night of the Hiroshima Commemoration, Dharma Cloud Temple in the Upper Hamlet was quietly bathed in golden candle glow. First to speak was Phap Anh, a monk in his fifties who told his childhood story–the trauma of American tanks arriving in his front yard at sunset one morning when he was a little boy. Ever since that day, whenever he watches a sunset, he said, his eyes fill with tears. He told how soothing the practice of mindfulness had been to heal the wounds of war. Still, his tears come at sunset.

Then it was my turn. Someone handed me a microphone. The natural compassion of the audience and the anchor of my own breath helped me tell the murder story without breaking down. Lucy was hearing it for the first time in the company of several hundred people. Thank God she heard it first in the womb of Plum Village.

Then one of the guests from the Middle East told her tale of war and personal redemption. This was the first Plum Village retreat where both Israelis and Palestinians had come together for reconciliation: the air was charged with the weight of war and mutual oppression. But by the end of the retreat, I saw Israelis and Palestinians with their arms around each other–Palestinians chucking baby Israelis on their chins. And I witnessed the former enemies joined in song.

That night we remembered–we remembered the bombs on Hiroshima that were dropped when I was two years old. We acknowledged the weight of the damage to the earth and her beings, the scope of the suffering of violence and combat that I felt had somehow erupted into the death of my own family. That "…rough beast slouching…" down the decades. In the darkness of our grieving, we were given a little light. Monks handed each of us a candle–each lit by the flame before it–to carry in procession, hundreds of us, outdoors, circling the lotus pond–breathing, stepping gently on the earth–toward a pure, white stone Buddha about five feet tall, seated under a tree in the darkened garden. With every step, I chanted to myself, "Forgive, forgive, forgive…."

Mute, we placed our candles at the Buddha's feet, making a conflagration of peace, lowering ourselves to the earth where we sat without a word, our hearts on fire.

FIREKEEPER

Love in its essence is spiritual fire.

—Emanuel Swedenborg

Not until twelve years after the fact did I feel strong enough to deal with the gruesome particulars of the crime. I was ready to dig up answers to my questions, to unfold another layer of my grief.

I drove to Pennsylvania from North Carolina, made an appointment with the district attorney who had handled the crime, entered the stacks of the Coyne County Courthouse to exercise my right to public information. Charles's defense attorney refused to see me. Even though he had died, she was still bound by client confidentiality.

My hands shook as I scanned the police records, the court reports, as I came face to face with the gruesome details of Charles Grand's bloody rampage that ended my family members' lives. Absorbing far too many gruesome details, I read Grand's account of the murders as told to his girlfriend who, after sitting and listening to every gory moment of what he did, had gone straight to the police. Because of my research, I have the dubious designation of *family holder of the particulars* of the murders. Could this be anything like a native lineage holder? Firekeeper?

Ours was the first DNA case in the jurisdiction, which in itself made it big news. According to DNA evidence, nineteen-year-old Charles Grand, son of the man who said, "We'll get whoever did this," neighbor and longtime friend of the family, was indeed the murderer. It was only then that I learned that Charles's girlfriend was videotaped claiming Charles planned to go back and murder his parents and grandmother. So our murders were only a rehearsal. Dear God.

I had not attended the trial; I had not listened to the TV accounts; I had not read the newspapers. All the details were new. I sat in the corner of the County Records Department sobbing. At the time all I knew was that Connie, Allen and Bobby had been "bludgeoned and stabbed" to death. And that other deep horror, that Connie had been raped. Now I wanted to know more. My questions were legion: Exactly how did this boy kill my widowed sister-in-law and my two nephews? Were drugs involved? How did he get into the house? Where did he get the murder weapons? In what order did he murder them? How long and in what ways did they suffer? Even more importantly, why? Why did this boy take his friend Allen's life and the life of Allen's mother and brother? Asking these questions became a way of laying hands on my emotions, of coming face to face with the suffering, of taking charge of the next step in my healing.

Some teachers say you don't come to Zen until you have suffered enough. My suffering was a fire; I was ready to tend it. And so I learned the word *loving-kindness* that is two words in English but one among Buddhists. I learned not only the word but also a way of letting loving-kindness drop into my body, my heart. Day by day. Through watching my breath. Through cultivating silence. Through the only antidote to cruelty: mindful attention.

The words of the Buddha slowly entered me through the conduit of my teacher, Thich Nhat Hanh: *Regard the pond: identify with the frog as well as the fly, the predator as well as the victim. There is no self and other.*

My epiphany of forgiveness came like an earthquake–at once painful and joyful, holy and profane–changing the way I look at myself, at everyone and everything.

In Zen, there is no word for forgiveness. In the here and now, we have dropped our separate self. There is no self to forgive and no other to be forgiven. Who is the one to be forgiven? And who is the one to forgive? *The one who bows and the one who is bowed to are both by nature empty. Therefore, the communication between them is inexpressibly perfect.*

Zen practice is full of paradox. The Soto Zen ancestor Dogen-Zenji uttered this verse, repeated in meditation halls around the world:

To study the Buddha way is to study the self;
to study the self is to forget the self;
to forget the self is to be enlightened by all things;
to be enlightened by all things

is to be liberated from one's own body and mind
and those of others
such that no trace of enlightenment remains.
Yet that tracelessness endures.

What we call emptiness in Zen is anything but empty in our usual sense of the word. Emtpiness is full of everything. Emptiness manifests most easily in my life with children. I sit with one of my grand-children, look into her eyes, and I see the child in me. Both of us are awake in the moment. When I am with a child is when I am most "at play in the fields of the Lord"–guileless, joyful, unassuming. The two of us are equally empty. Empty of what? Empty of a separate self. So in Zen, emptiness is the beautiful bowl that holds everything! Impeccable communica-tion. I and my grandchild, we *inter-are*.

How dare I, then, write a book about Zen and forgiveness? All we need do is practice the kindness and care taught by Buddha and Jesus, and there will be no necessity to forgive. Ah, but most of us still live on what author Sara Jenkins calls *this side* of nir-vana. On this side of nirvana lurk murders and aban-donments, betrayals and abuse. The seeds of grief and hurt and resentment and woundedness are cultivated in ways that seem to originate not from inside our selves but from somewhere outside. We often feel we lack control of our lives. Like seeds in the wind, we're buffeted about, who knows where to land.

We sometimes–no, often–feel like victims. Certainly I felt like a victim of the murders. As a young adult, I hungrily gulped Truman Capote's

In Cold Blood about the farm family murdered in Kansas. I was part of the culture that feeds–and feeds upon—a kind of blood lust, resentment and anger. In our love-hate relationship with the media, we grab a tragedy and pound on it, analyze it, drag it out, report upon it, send it out on facebook, dramatize it, broadcast it, make documentaries and films that rehearse the violence. But our hatred has the capacity to destroy us.

Here we are, the victims of suffering and trauma and violence–smoldering, burning. Will we be consumed? Or do we have a chance to raise ourselves from the ashes? I deeply believe this human life is an opportunity to realize what Jesus knew when he said, *You are the light of the world,* or to realize what Buddha meant when he said *Dwell. You are the light itself.* This burning in the fire of life: why can't we find liberation right here? What are we here for if not to wake up?

The Taoist teacher Derek Lin tells a story, in which I have changed the genders, about the wise one who hands her student an empty sack and a basket of potatoes, and asks the student to think of all who have recently done her wrong. For each person you cannot forgive, says the teacher, carve a name on the potato and place the potato into the sack. Soon the student's sack is full. Carry the sack with you for a week wherever you go, instructs the master. Easy, thinks the student. But, alas, she is wrong.

Day after day, the sack becomes heavier until after a time as the cut potatoes rot, they stink like a sewer. Still the student manages to carry the bag with her all week. At the end of the week, the master asks her what she has learned.

When we can't forgive others, we carry our resentments like a heavy bag of stinking spuds, she says.

Yes, rot is what comes from holding a grudge, says the sage. How can you lighten your load?

Try to forgive, says the student. Then I can remove those potatoes that represent the folks I can forgive? Actually, I'm ready to forgive them all, she adds. The teacher instructs her to go ahead and remove the potatoes. Later the sage asks, This week while you were carrying the bag around, did anyone wrong you?

The student thinks it over and admits that indeed there were some people who had treated her badly. At the same time, her heart sinks when she thinks of having to refill the bag. Then she asks the master a question: If there will always be those who wrong us, what good is the forgiveness teaching?

The master answers, My dear student, you are not yet in the realm of the Tao. Dropping the potatoes is the common approach to forgiveness, what most philosophies and religions teach: *strive to attain forgiveness.* This is not the Tao, because with the Tao, there's nothing to attain.

Then what is the Tao? Asks the student. Well, counters the teacher, if the potatoes are negative feelings, what does the bag represent? Let's see, the student hesitates. It is that which holds offense, my ego, my separate self! And if you let go of your separate self? Asks the teacher. What will happen? The hurts won't be so magnified, won't bother me, she answers. So, states the teacher, nothing to carry around, no more rotten odors. The Tao of forgiveness tells us not just to remove the potatoes, but to put down the bag, too. Therefore, my dear student, forgiveness takes no effort at all.

In our tradition of Zen practice, we first learn to be gentle with ourselves. We learn to recognize our deepest negative emotions, to care for them as if they were our children, to hug them, to treat them with kindness, and thus to transform them into forgiveness, happiness, joy. I found out that my problem with the boy who murdered my family was not with who he was, but with my *not understanding who he was.*

In each of us, no matter whom, lives a Buddha, or divine nature. We bury our divine nature under layers of forgetting. Here's a mundane example: at work, her co-workers see Sally as the office barracuda, manipulating everyone, lying, cheating to get ahead, and pretending all the while that she is a kind and virtuous woman.

Looking deeply, we discover that Sally's cover-up began when she was mistreated at the hands of her father as a child. She has learned to survive by doing whatever she can to succeed, even if this means trampling others in her wake. Every day, she commits "little murders." It is hard to see Sally's Buddha nature. But because most people do not see her Buddha nature does not mean it does not exist.

For a long time before the murders, I had known the act of forgiveness freed me, but I did not yet understand how it could free not only those I pardoned, but my mother, father, and ancestors as well. Even the murderer himself. You see, I saw myself as separate. Nor did I really know how to pardon. I had learned only to take the potatoes out of my sack, not yet to put down the bag. My potatoes continued to multiply, almost as if I were cultivating them. The sack of my separate self was still intact.

Before he died, ten years after I became a student of Zen, Daddy asked me to help him forgive his mother for repeatedly beating him with a trunk strap when he was a child. In this way, I knew that *he* knew I had forgiven *him*. Having Daddy ask me for advice was a small miracle. My father, who had always been hypercritical of what he saw as my "artsy-fartsy hippie" lifestyle, ethics and politics, actually had come to regard me as an adept in the art of forgiveness.

While in Zen we do not often hear the word *forgiveness*, we do hear in

countless Buddhist sutras and teachings the words compassion and *loving-kindness* and *transformation*–teachings that demonstrate a patience and benevolence toward all beings—a love finer than mother-love. Because this love does not cling, it is free from attachment. We can feel the perfect wisdom born of understanding. We learn to listen to our breath not because we want to achieve anything, but because at first we want relief from our suffering. Along the way come opportunities for us to gather new tools–skillful means–for manifesting mindful attention, compassion, forgiveness and care. We learn to engage with others in ways that nourish kindness in the world. As one of our morning chants goes: "Bring joy to one person in the morning and relieve another's grief in the afternoon."

Why has my back always had to be smack against the wall for me to receive the real teachings of life? I have always had to hit bottom or have a breakdown–breaking down of the old, I suppose–to make way for the new. Not that I recommend this way of learning. But isn't it what we make of our suffering? Does the lotus grow in clear water? No, only in the mud.

Time is short. Today could be our last day together. Out of the desperation of the murders, I was finally ready to learn how to listen deeply to my partner and my parents and my children–to listen so intently that sometimes I can drop all distinction between subject and object. I have come to know that my actions are my only true belongings. And hardest of all, I have learned that the way out of suffering is to walk straight into the fire. We must come face to face with suffering. It was only by so doing that I could experience the clear heart of pardon, for myself and others. No distinction. It was in the fire of losing three people to homicide in one horrifying night that finally I could put down not only the potatoes of my resentment and anger, but the very sack of separateness that had held them for so long.

TO SEIZE THE FIRE

What the hand dare seize the fire?
And what shoulder and what art
Could twist the sinews of thy heart?

—William Blake, "The Tyger"

The need to forgive burns in me. If this is true for others, the act of forgiveness ignites in us an action which ultimately cleans and purifies our karma, scours us out. Who dares touch the energy of the fire of forgiveness? And furthermore, who made this fire? Where did the "other" come from? What is the source of our suffering? Perhaps these are questions best left unasked until we learn how to deal with our suffering. The Buddha said: I teach only two things—suffering and the cessation of suffering. He did not speculate as to the beginning of time or the origin of evil or what we become after we die. He taught us to deal with life on life's terms in the present moment.

I was long caught in judging myself and others. I tried not to do so, still I try. Once years ago, I tried even to the point of placing a rubber band on my wrist and snapping it every time I made a judgment. My wrist was sore. I had learned that judging others is counterproductive and counter-expansive. How can I thoroughly love those I judge? Yet I still catch myself. The ego persists in staking its claim; the ego wants to separate me from others, to keep its precious false belief that I am I and you are you and never the twain shall meet. It is busy trying to divide or vilify and solidify "the other."

This is what sells newspapers. Bad news. Gossip. Retribution. We thrive on these. We are natural born *shit detectors* partly because our brains are hard-wired to look for the enemy in order to protect ourselves. If we can sniff out the predator, we are more apt to stay alive in this moment. *What was that rustle in the leaves? Stay alert! Look around you!* This is the hyper-vigilance of the lookout tower of the limbic brain. It is only when I come to realize again and again—and perhaps now my heart must speak to my brain—that there is no separate self, and that I am an integral part of all that is, that I am able to relax all my illusory divisions and truly forgive.

What exactly do we have in the present moment? Scraps of anger left over from our childhood that threaten to disarm and confuse us? The crud of old resentments? Residue of betrayal? How do we begin to drop these? One way I have discovered to drop these stale emotions is to drop my separate self that engages with them. That is, I do what my first teacher, Dai-En Bennage, suggested—sit down and shut up.

I sit, I drop my (separate) self and I am immediately in the middle–Paradise. There is no waiting!

However, this Ideal takes training. So let me begin–when else to begin?—in this moment. I relax my belly and take three conscious, unhindered inhalations, giving back three conscious unhindered exhalations. Suddenly the light is brighter. I notice the sunshine on green oak leaves, their subtle colors, the dance of the branches in a light July breeze, passing clouds, the photos of my dear beloveds on my desk top, my cold feet, my aching computer shoulders, and I am Here, Now. This!

The act of letting go wipes out even the need to forgive. Now I exist in a state of loving-kindness and non-attachment, glimpses of which I receive in meditation or sometimes in the woods. Yesterday, walking with my dogs through clouds in the mountain forest, with millions of white rhododendron blossoms lighting up the earth and thrown at our feet, I let go. Or listening to Philip play a wistful Billy Strayhorn tune on the piano, I can let go.

And so I have found a way of forgiving the past by entering the present. The burden of past and future no longer holds me down. The present moment is light and unfettered. It is *what is*. And nine-hundred and ninety-nine times out of a thousand, this moment is at worst neutral and at best actually pleasant, because it is unfettered. I think of the chains of Dickens' Ghost of Christmas Past, the perpetual drag of the heavy iron links. Here Dickens gives us a fine metaphor for what we do to make ourselves suffer.

As a young woman, I lived much of the time in the burdensome past or the frightening future, drunk with rage and self-loathing. No wonder I was agitated. Once I heard Thich Nhat Hanh answer the question, "Where do we go when we die?" by asking another question: "Why contemplate the future when we do not yet know how to take care of ourselves in the present?" This is like asking the child's question, "Where does the fire come from?" Buckminster Fuller answered: "It is the sun unfurling itself from the log." It is the ever-forgiving sun within the ever-forgiving tree, both shining the light of their mindfulness for all to see. Once again, forgiveness comes through our simple attention to the present moment. Breathing in, I know I am breathing in. Breathing out, I know I am breathing out.

What of the real or imagined hurts that will not go out on the breath? I am holding one, now, that has lasted all night and into the morning, all the way through morning meditation. I need to walk in the shoes of the woman who has made me suffer. I need to quiet myself again, in order to look deeply to understand her suffering, which is not unlike my own. I am looking at her shaky health, at her non-existent family life, at her shattered friendships. I am looking at her body, how she carries herself. I am looking now beyond appearances. I adopt the eye of a seer, and see into her past. Just as many of my own difficulties stem from childhood, so must hers. While I may not know about her childhood, I do know, because with the energy of love, I can sense the trouble that brewed there and is manifest in the present moment. I can sense the trouble that started even before she was born, in this person's ancestry, just as I inherited a rich stream of trouble and joy from my own colorful lineage. This is no academic experiment. It happens at the level of heart and gut.

First I walk and breathe, walk and breathe, to take care of my anger. Then immediately I write her an email which I mindfully decline to send. I put it in Drafts on my computer program. Eventually, now that I have looked deeply enough into her, I see myself. I know I will delete the email. Poof! The flame of anger unfurls itself from cyberspace. It is far too easy, with a single click, to send a nasty or blaming email. My habit is to put them in Drafts. Sometimes I need to go through the process of briefly expressing the anger, though, careful not to rehearse it, before sending the civil email that states only the bare minimum, with words that throw straw on the mud: forgetting any praise or blame, sticking to "I" messages, suggesting we meet for tea. The supposed perpetrator of my hurt only remains the "other" until I calm myself and begin to look beyond the incident at hand into her deepest recesses. What hand dare seize the fire?

The second level of total forgiveness is to identify the quality in me that I dislike in her. I see clearly that I have that quality, which in this case is my need to control events and their outcomes. Now I look deeply into my own life and my own ancestry. Because before I complete this level, the process of forgiveness is unfinished. I think of ways in which I have acted out similarly to the incident in question. I ask why I want to hold onto my need to control. Oh, because I am afraid—afraid of what? Hmmm.

Afraid that if I let go of the reins, someone else will be in charge. Yet I need to let go of the illusion that I must control my destiny or else someone else will. The Tao Te Ching, that great relinquisher, tells us that she who controls others may be powerful, but she who has mastered herself is mightier still. What shoulder and what art could twist the sinews of the heart?

And finally, in the final phase of forgiveness, I make a date with her for tea. Without blaming, without even needing to refer to the incident in question, I listen to her. I listen to what she says that lives in the spaces between her words. I watch her body language. My whole purpose in inviting her to tea is to listen. And for the two of us to begin anew. If she brings up the negative incident, I might ask her a non-blaming question, such as, "How do you feel about what happened between us?" to better understand.

It is possible that the person with whom we wish to reconcile will not accept our invitation to tea. And that is all right. I have swept my own sidewalk. If within me there is a residue of resentment or complaint toward her—I, myself am not ready for tea, either–I return to my breath and ask myself what in me has a need to grasp or hold onto this negativity? Oh yes, the brain again. It is organic and natural for me to grab hold of fear. In mindfulness that I am no longer a cave dweller in the time of dinosaurs, that I am not on the battlefield of any war, I can let the trouble go, truly let it go.

In the world of interbeing, there are no enemies. Within our own bodies, why would we need to "fight" cancer? Fighting a cold, fighting a disease that is inside of my body, one that is most likely a form of inflammation (another kind of burning) seems to me a waste of my energy. Like my anger, I believe any bodily sickness is, as the poet, Rilke put it, the illusion of a fire-breathing dragon that is really a princess in distress, crying out for help from me. So instead of fighting it and getting burned, perhaps I can ask it, "What do you need from me, my dear sickness?" The same goes for judgment. "What do you need from me, my dear judgment?" Often when I give myself a time in meditation to ask such questions, the answers are wise and beneficial, coming as they do from my inner Buddha. And if I can forestall judgment, i.e., separation, I can forestall dis-ease. Forestalling means softening, yielding, learning to love.

Often when I ask my body what it needs from me, the answer will be, "I need you to let go." Sometimes the answer will be another question, such as, "Take a look at what you said to him yesterday. You were adamant. What were you really feeling? What was underneath your words?" Here is the wise and benevolent observer who has only my best interests at heart, who never judges me, would never condemn me. The one who asks the questions is the one who knows.

Then from the ashes of judgment and separation and vilification comes new life. "As the dust of fear and anxiety settles," says one of our morning chants, "with open heart, one-pointed mind, we turn to the three jewels"—Buddha, Dharma, Sangha—in whom, in which, there is no division. As in God.

We separate ourselves by name, clan, town, state, country and continent, religion, race, politics, preferences: "like" and "don't like" on facebook. We break things down, we split them, which always reminds me of Plato's comic poet Mephistopheles telling the story of how Zeus grew jealous of the original beings who were round, androgynous and multi-talented. In a rage, Zeus harnessed lightning bolts to split them in two. We break down. We form opinions. We even split the poor atom, wreaking havoc. And we have used up our best minds to do these things.

What I propose is that we harness the world's best minds, young and old, here and now, and charge them with the creative task of uniting us as a planet. We are, still, all in the same little battered blue boat, "our dear fucked up planet," as Henry Miller called it, rowing in circles through space. Shall we not, then, row together, and merrily?

FALLING OPEN: THE PRACTICE OF FORGIVENESS

...flames

in our veins, run

their hot red track...

to whet

our bursting souls against the bark

of time...

—M.C. Richards

Let my life unfold and fall open like a flower—innocent, joyful, free. The new paradigm, in which the practice of forgiveness flows freely, is the paradigm of *interconnection*. If I know deeply, as the Buddha taught, that we are not one and not two, but that we inter-are, how can I hold onto any feelings of betrayal? My ego is not even a separate ego. Nothing is wholly mine. Why would I want to own a resentment? In the light of interbeing, how could I feel attached to or possessive of anything or anyone? In the light of interbeing, my anger falls away like dust off the petal of an opening rose.

In the petal exists the whole flower. One small resentment fading away represents the way of peace–all our little purposes lost in the great design. The macrocosm lives in the microcosm. Finding peace in one's self, we find peace in the world. In my inner being exists a universal potential that springs from the root of a tree called life, manifesting in all things.

Life is a kind of dream. We give to and receive from the hours and days what we do not know we know. Entering the inner life, we weave the facts and minutiae of our days with the light that comes from within. We engage head, hands and heart in all we do. I recall the story of the potter who says it is not the pot she is forming, but what lies within. She is absorbed only in what remains when the pot is broken. Love is what remains of my dear murdered family.

I think, too, of the broken relationship with my brother. What lies within this brokenness for me? Light, light seeping through the cracks. The spirit of the form of our relationship is still alive—the breath of the form that was our sibling life. Even more poignantly, I do not wish to rehearse my anger. The one time I rehearsed my anger with my brother was the last time he spoke to me—more than eight years ago. Our broken relationship is in part the fruit of my anger. And yet because it is broken, a light can shine in.

Like day lily buds, our bodies open from the inside. Inside of me–when I fully realize my interconnection with my brother–is no judgment of myself or him, only the continual opening. I was once, and far too long, betrayed by my own inner judge. There was a constant critical voice of authority. The person I truly betrayed was myself. Now on the far side of that betrayal, I want to encourage in myself and others a life of mystery, awe, wonder and joy.

Each day I want to rediscover, to recover, the mind of the child, beginner's mind, to find the little miracles within and without. I want to relax into the rhythms of sun and moon, sleeping and waking, breathing and heartbeat. I want to catch moments like fireflies: the hollow rat-a-tat-tat of the pileated woodpecker in our tree, the mist over the mountains, the high speckled notes of a jazz riff played by Philip in the other room, the dog snoring. Then let them go as they came. I cannot force spiritual perception: it manifests only when conditions are right. I can only plough the ground with my daily practice, through returning again and again to my breath–the open door to the heart, to mindfulness.

It is more important to the practice of forgiveness that I *be*, rather than that I *see*. That is, the quality and consistency of my mindfulness determines the quality of my understanding and awakening. We go within in the early part of the day, to prepare ourselves to see in a more focused way the outer universe with its glad surprises. I learn to listen to my intuition, the still small voice, the dharmic teacher within. Sometimes all I have is a question. In the fullness of inner time, an answer grows. Compassion flowers.

My ability to *be* in a way that fosters forgiveness depends on living in community. To be is to inter-be. And I cannot inter-be without the full base of the practice community. To a true student, Sangha is everywhere apparent. To have been affiliated with the Order of Interbeing and its international garden of Sanghas for over twenty years has made me part of an altogether interdependent way of life, inspired by our teacher, Thich Nhat Hanh. He gives us two important tools. First, he tells us Sangha building or community building is our most salient work. Secondly he asks us to remember and bring to the Sangha all our relations: to realize every moment that we live in the envelope of our blood ancestors and our spiritual ancestors, our blood children and our spiritual children. Then how can we ever hold fast to resentments and thoughts of retribution? The community would break. Happiness, I have learned, is not an individual affair.

No one person can fully meet our expectations. So to love one another means to honor, respect and accept each other *as is*. We are more apt to behave this way with family members—to say that Dad will be Dad and let it go at that. But with others, if we do not perceive others as related to us, we see them as imperfect and therefore we do not accept their company. Followed to the extreme, this method would lead to our total isolation from the human family. So we learn to accept everyone as our sister, our brother. Inclusiveness. And with that acceptance, forgiveness flows. It is the milk of human kindness.

Sometimes my efforts to throw straw on the mud, (the letter, joining the other for tea) to make a path for reconciliation, do not bear fruit. I invite the person for tea, and we have a sort of beginning anew, but still they go away and do not come back. I ask many questions. We listen. What led up to the hurtful incident? What feelings of insecurity or fear are at the root of our encounter? For what do I need to apologize? How can I come to a place of compassion for you now? Sometimes the other person is not ready to touch the pain that was triggered for them by our encounter. Of course, the purpose of reconciliation is not to place blame. The purpose is to listen deeply to one another, to find the roots of our pain, find our affinities. Still, the reality is that people come and people go as the cells of our bodies slough off in the mutable ecology of brotherhood and sisterhood. We need not resist the changes. In any case, we have become teachers and students to one another through sharing our experiences. Anyone who lives in community can tell you that folks come and go. When a person who visited Cloud Cottage to practice with us only once tells me years later that they were touched in a life-changing way by that hour and a half of mindfulness—to see that such a community is possible—I realize again that not everyone has to stay. Visitors can take what they like and incorporate it into their own lives, perhaps in another community.

We teach by example. Within the Sangha we try to understand one another's diverse temperaments, to work with them and through them, rather than against them. We do not wish to make clones of ourselves. We celebrate differences and individual talents. One Sangha member can dance. She teaches us to dance. One Sangha member can paint. We attend her art openings. Another works at the local hospital. We are invited to train the hospital staff in mindfulness. Yet another can cook. He brings his food to share.

One Sangha member, Laurie Serfas, put it this way, combining her words with our teacher's:

Cloud Cottage—our community—our sangha, is a garden full of many varieties of beautiful individuals. And like the trees and flowers of a garden, some individuals may bloom early in the bright sunshine, opening their petals wide in vibrant color. Others in our garden may prefer the cover of shade, patiently gathering nutrients to bloom later in the season. Some individuals in the garden may bear many fruits while others may offer cool shade.

No one individual is greater than, less than, or the same as any other individual in our garden. Each member of our sangha has unique gifts to offer to the community. And we each have areas that need care and attention as well. When we are mindful and can recognize and appreciate each member's contribution and see our weaknesses as potential for growth, we learn to live together in harmony.

We ask, "What are the gifts of this person and how can we help them flower?" Then, within the Sangha, we enjoy a united, organic, interacting whole, where—just as our teacher keeps photos of his monks and nuns before him–many of us visualize each other's faces in our morning meditations, holding one another in the light.

To live in such a way is revolutionary. We take the risk of loving and accepting and forgiving one another in a nonpossessive way, bringing folks together to build something that feels both tangible and spiritual. We are alive and unique humans connected in purpose with all that is, working for all beings, warm in our relations and clear in our way of seeing. In this Information Age, if we can go within and learn to be open enough to see, perhaps we will not only survive the onslaught of information, but find our connection with it.

Often we take turns sitting in the front during Thay's Dharma talks. Once during a Dharma talk at Deer Park Monastery, when it was my turn to sit in the front row, Thay made eye contact with me as he was teaching, and kept his eyes deeply riveted on me for half an hour. I was so happy to have his full attention, but I wondered why, when there were so many hundreds of people present, that he was teaching me directly. Did he feel I needed most what he had to say? Later, I read that this is how Thay practices interbeing with various members of his Sangha.

To have brought the Order of Interbeing to the West was as if Thay kissed Sleeping Beauty. I was one of the sleepers, and this community, sprung from the killing fields of Vietnam to foster world peace, formed something larger than itself, and changed everything for me. Everything changes. Nothing is lost.

LETTER TO THE KILLER

Dear Charles,

It is 2011—twenty-one years since you killed Connie, Allen and Bobby. I talked with your mother twelve years hence, and we cried together for our lost children—her child, my sister-in-law and two precious nephews. We still do not know what twisted you to such an extent that you turned on your neighbors and friends. Your bloody act was vicious, depraved. You must have been a lonely and tormented child.

The dark stone you threw into our pool caused endless ripples. Because of what you did, an untold number of people were bereft. Connie, Bobby and Allen were deeply loved and needed. I cannot bear to imagine their last horrible moments on this earth. You took them from us, and for that you paid and we paid. Your parents and grandmother were left with nothing. You were their only child. We sobbed and mourned and still we do–Connie's sisters, her brother, Mark and my daughters and so many others. You took away the only grandchildren of Bobby's and Allen's paternal grandparents. You piled loss upon loss.

In desperation, I sought help in Zen. I entered the practice with an intensity and determination that saw me through days when I did not want to sit on a cushion. But I had found a new clarity and light, and some relief from my grief. So I sat...and sat, in the silence, counting my breaths for five years.

Although I did not set out to do so, amazingly, I spontaneously forgave you, Charles. Somehow, suddenly I understood how completely out of control you had to be. The monster that killed my family was not the whole of you. Almost unbelievably, I knew that you and I were not one and not two, but that we inter-are. This experience changed my life–that I was able to see you as myself—that I was able to see the murderer in myself and forgive you even when you would not, or could not, forgive yourself.

Still I was afraid to meet you in person to tell you so. And I knew you were in hell. Did you ever receive the loving energy I sent on wings of prayer so many days, holding you in the arms of my imagination?

Then you took your own life. Your suicide brought the entire grief home again to me. If I had had the courage to say *I forgive you* in person, would that have saved you? Would you still have hung yourself to death, knowing that at least one person cared?

Charles, there is no way out of paying for this deep karmic gash. Yet the Buddha was able to forgive even the mass murderer Angulimala, who wore a brazen necklace of the finger bones of his victims. The Buddha showed us that no crime is unforgiveable. He ordained the penitent Angulimala as one of his monks. Jesus said on the cross, "Forgive them, Father, for they know not what they do." You are forgiven. Yet our karma must be purified, and that, Charles, takes some doing, as I know from my own short life this time around. The seeds we have planted will come to fruition either now or in subsequent lifetimes.

My deepest hope for you is that wherever your consciousness resides, you are free, and that you are able to plant seeds of love there. Or, if your consciousness is no more, let me begin to sow the seeds of peace on behalf of you and the dead.

In honor of Connie, Allen and Bobby and all beings...

Judith

AFTERWORD

Consummatum Est

—for the lost girls and boys

If God is fire and I am burning wood
I ask but that I burn without a trace.
Along the way may I be wood that's good
That I might cast some light upon the face
Of one whose suffering's deeper far than mine—
The girl whose wound or boy whose scar's so deep
That scarring disallows dear love to shine.
Misfortune's child's the one with whom I cry
Whose tears extinguish harmony and peace.
I hold her hand and meet her eye to eye
That somehow in fire's stoking pain might cease.
Oh, burn the years before I may expire
In unity of life and death as fire.

—Judith Toy

This is a plea for forgiveness to those who believe this book should not have been written and published. You may be right. Over many years as I weighed the potential assets versus the liabilities of publicly sharing my story, with the names changed to protect the family from further publicity, the plusses soon outweighed the minuses. How could I have predicted that another loss would befall us even as I carried on with this difficult project—that our son James would suddenly die? In the wake of this loss, work on the manuscript stalled for three years, until the book called me back so urgently that I knew I must pick up enough of the pieces in order to continue.

In the early days of the writing and research, most of our friends encouraged me. When I tried to talk with family, there were times I was shunned. Mark was wary yet supportive. With good reason, I was judged by others in the family an opportunist. I did not attempt to call Connie and Mark's mother, Hazel. The very idea felt like a hot potato. When I called the church where Connie and the boys were active, the minister ignored my calls. When I phoned Connie's sister, Fanny, to talk about Connie in light of this project, Fanny never spoke to me again. We had once been sisters-in-law, always friends. But clearly, either the pain was too great for her to share with me, or she believes that I am dishonoring Connie's memory–or both. All of this is really conjecture, because there has been only the silence. This has led me to ponder: *how much of our suffering stems from undelivered communications?*

No words convey the hurt my family has suffered. Others in our family as well as outside of it do not believe in forgiving what they deem the unforgiveable. To these I say I do not excuse the act; but I can forgive the actor. There is no attitude we can take, no opinion we can make, that will bring Connie, Bobby and Allen back to this life. While transformation is possible, the popular notion of "closure" is a myth. These events, once committed, will always be with us. Yet if we are unwilling to forgive, with what are we left? The unwillingness to forgive. Only the angry threads of our rage and despair.

Perhaps some of the family feels about me the way I first felt about Willow, the psychic, who read in the news about Connie and the boys. When Mark believed her "messages from the dead," I thought him a fool. Out of my own wounds, I was quick to judge, to see her as a fraud. Now these many years later, after learning that mindfulness leads to insight, insight fosters understanding, and the fruit of understanding is always compassion–my eyes have been opened. I can look with my heart. I can see what solace Willow offered Mark and Lane. Indeed, who other than Willow would have dared move into the murder house? Ironically, for me, Willow's son married Lane's sister, to become the loving father of her two children. My dear family, please forgive me.

We do not often think of the victims among the families of the perpetrators. Strangely, as my interview with her confirmed, the mother of the boy who committed the crimes was amazed and grateful to get my call. When Trina Grand said, "I am looking out my window at Connie's house right now," I felt a chill. But as I have learned through my work with groups such as People of Faith Against the Death Penalty and Murder Victims' Families for Reconciliation, the suffering of the families of the perpetrators is not less intense than the families of the victims. They become pariahs, outcasts. Furthermore, hardly anyone recognizes the emotional drain on the attorneys for both the prosecution and the defense. I have taught mindfulness meditation and total relaxation to attorneys who work on death row in North Carolina. I found them exhausted and depleted at the end of a year that tallied eight deaths by lethal injection.

I have learned and relearned that blame is only a way to deflect my own feelings–that it is not so much what happens to us as how we ultimately respond. Blaming makes me part of the problem. When I forgive, I live in the solution. Our friend and Dharma teacher, Roger Hawkins, speaks of how, in every moment, we are welcomed unconditionally by the universe. If only we will wake up to this. If only we will walk into the open, waiting arms of love. In the aftermath of the tragedy of the murders, I was able to open the mysterious, hidden gift of love inside the horror. Thich Nhat Hanh puts it another way: nowhere is the Buddha so close as in our deepest suffering.

And speaking of buddhas, this is to thank my darling Philip for hours of editing and emotional balance. For never leaving my side. Some of the family was, understandably, deeply distressed upon the release of the kickstarter.com video to raise funds for this book. They were afraid that our young grandchildren would happen upon the gruesome story by accident. Philip wrote to them this letter:

Dear Family,

I know I am only guessing at your upset over this project. Nevertheless, I do respect and honor whatever the root cause of that upset may be. Just as I honor and respect Judith every inch of the way on the long and difficult road of this endeavor.

Starting with the sudden death of my 29-year-old sister and surrogate mother, Viola Mae, and her unnamed infant son, and ending with my son James' sudden tragic passing—my own lifelong grief is teaching me that eventually it has to be shared. In that tough sharing is the stuff of liberation and waking up. It is only here on the path of understanding and compassion for all beings that this book can come to fruition. It represents a major milestone in both Judith's mindfulness and recovery practices—mine, too, by association—of growth in love and service.

When I speak about James and his death I know I am not only healing myself but in some very real ways—many of which I may never fully understand—I am healing my brothers and sisters. It is in this light that Murder as a Call to Love—*the initial fundraising video, the writing, the marketing, the book and beyond—must be seen. It has a dignity and a dynamic that is larger than we who tell it. With this book, Judith heals and describes her healing and forgiveness to the world at large. It is a calling for both of us, one that has lasted for years, and I am grateful for it as a means to fulfilling my own best vows and wishes.*

So, darlings, you, too, can heal some of your grief on this same bold road, and perhaps find a special kind of feeling for your Judith–her work, her life and her path. The very last thing she would wish is to hurt you.

Lovingly, only lovingly,

Philip

GRATITUDES

He who sits by the fire, thankless for
the fire, is just as if he had no fire.

—W.J. Cameron

First things first: to my husband and spiritual
brother Philip, how could I have finished this project
without you? For your endless patience and skillful
editing and marketing, and for stoking the fire of this
book through the years, a kiss. I carry your heart in
my heart. To my teacher, the Venerable Thich Nhat
Hanh, I hold your hand wherever I go. (To think
that you got into trouble as a teen monk for writing
these words on the temple pillar: *For all beings*!) To
my mother Marjorie for her unswerving steadiness,
and my wondrous daughters, my best friends, and
to my stepsons and grandchildren, you lend me the
strength. And thank you, too, Mark. For our small
spiritual family at Cloud Cottage, you always catch
me in your embrace, and for this I am thankful. You

have been my safety net, the Net of Indra. To our expanding global family of the Order of Interbeing (OI), I touch the earth. To those many of you who choose to remain anonymous (and you know who you are), thank you for holding me. You are my freedom sangha, one day at a time. To Jane A., Karen F. and Nan J., you know. To Cloud Cottage Editions' first author, Dharma friend and backer Roger Shikan Hawkins, we give our profound thanks. To TV producer and filmmaker, Cinammon Kennedy, for shooting and producing the kickstarter video, wow, thank you, dear heart. Bless you, kickstarter. com. To Larry and Linda Cammarata, a smile, for offering first. Many bows to Tina and Aram Dadian for always giving me a room. To my editors, including Susan Hadler, Melvin McLeod, Carl Jerome, Tynette Deveaux, Leslie Rawls, Sandi Tomlin-Sutker, Natascha Bruckner, Janelle Combelic and Sister Annabel Laity, thank you for making me a better writer. To my women's writing group, especially Sara Jenkins, my palms are joined. To Sara again, and to Cinnamon and John Kennedy, for reviewing the manuscript; to my advisory board—Sara Jenkins again, the late Asa Huggett, Greg Levoy, Robin Sierra, Dale Neal, Jacqueline Boyce, many smiles of thank-you.

I am deeply grateful to Dai-En Bennage, Sensei, Dharma teacher Lyn Fine, and Genro Lee Milton, Sensei, as well as Rev. Yayoi Matsumoto, for my early training in Zen: *Namu Dai Bosa*. Many thanks to senior OI Dharma teacher Richard Brady, who listens like Avalokitesvara. Thanks to Valerie Brown for protecting Old Path Sangha. A deep bow to folks like

Kobutsu Kevin Malone and Bo and Sita Lozoff for pioneering mindfulness and meditation in our prisons, paving the way for people like my husband and me to more readily enter the system with Dharma. Bo Lozoff points out that "America locks up more of its population that any other nation on Earth…. In 1970, there were fewer than 200,000 prisoners in the US. By 1999, California alone had nearly that many." Our country remains the world's leading jailer. As of 2008, there were 225,000,000 people incarcerated here, in both public and private prisons.

To those fifty-plus of you who were happy to ante up your hard-earned cash to crowd-fund this project, first through kickstarter.com, and then on your own, Philip and I honor you with utmost gratitude:

Jane Albers, Margie Allison, Julia Borg, Norma Bradley, Richard Brady, Linda and Larry Cammarata, Joanna and Victor Chernauskas, Kimberly Childs, Janelle Combelic, April Conner, Carol Czeczot, Tebbe and Suzannah Davis, Gerhilde Dickerman, Teresa Garland, Harrison Greene, Mary Ellen Griffin, Susan Hadler, Susan Hales, Roger Hawkins, Donald Katz, Cinnamon Kennedy, Sheila Klein, Rebecca Krantz, Nancy Jarema, Sara Jenkins, Chris Larson, Odile Laugier, Joe and Laura Lilly, Arthur McDonald, Norman and Michaelene McWhinney, Susanne Olbrich and members of Northern Lights Sangha, The Venerables Pannavati and Pannadipa, Bill Patterson, David Percival, Sheri A. Rosenthal, Maggie Schlubach, Janet Terwilliger, Suzanne Thierry, Marjorie Timms, my sweet mother Marjorie Van Epps, Steve Wall, Carole Wilson, Vicki Waciega,

Kathy Wallace, Joy Yackley, my kidney sister Carole Winokur-Zissman.

Begging your forgiveness, the many whose names should be here, but that I have only momentarily forgotten. Let us know. Your names will go in future editions.

RESOURCES & RECOMMENDED READING

Education is not filling a pail but the lighting of a fire.
–William Butler Yeats

A Short Reading List

A Few Related Books by Thich Nhat Hanh

Anger: Wisdom for Cooling the Flames

Be Free Where You Are (written for inmates)

Happiness: Essential Mindfulness Practices

Old Path White Clouds: Walking in the Footsteps of the Buddha

Peace is Every Step: The Path of Mindfulness in Everyday Life

The Heart of the Buddha's Teachings: Transforming Suffering Into Peace, Joy & Liberation

The Sun, My Heart

Books of Interest by Other Authors

At Hell's Gate, A Soldier's Journey, by Claude Anshin Thomas

Cutting Through Spiritual Materialism, by Chogyam Trungpa

Great Doubt: the Spirit of Self-Inquiry, by Roger Hawkins

Healing After Loss: Daily Meditations for Working Through Grief, by Martha Whitmore Hickman

Learning True Love: Practicing Buddhism in a Time of War, by Sister Chan Khong

Siddhartha, by Hermann Hesse

The Three Pillars of Zen, Teaching, Practice, and Enlightenment, by Roshi Philip Kapleau

This Side of Nirvana, Memoirs of a Spiritually Challenged Buddhist, by Sara Jenkins

Toward Wholeness, Rudolf Steiner Education in America, by M.C. Richards

Tuning In: Mindfulness in Teaching and Learning, ed. Richard Brady

We're All Doing Time, A Guide to Getting Free, by Bo Lozoff

Zen Mind, Beginner's Mind, by Shunryu Suzuki

Zen Seeds, Reflections of a Female Priest, by Shundo Aoyama, translated by

Patricia Dai-En Bennage

Online Contacts

Our home Sangha, Cloud Cottage www.cloudcottage.org

To access the world of Thich Nhat Hanh, and for an online directory of world-wide communities practicing in that tradition www.iamhome.org

For more books by Thich Nhat Hanh www.parallax.org

The Mindfulness Bell, the international quarterly for students of Thich Nhat Hanh

http://www.mindfulnessbell.org/index.php

People of Faith Against the Death Penalty www.pfadp.org

Murder Victims' Families for Reconciliation www.mvfr.org

Prison Ashram Project of Bo and Sita Lozoff, www.humankindness.org

A Campaign for Forgiveness Research supports scientific studies that can deepen our understanding of forgiveness and begin the process of building many different roads to reconciliation. www.forgiving.org

The Forgiveness Project, a UK-based charitable organization which explores forgiveness, reconciliation and conflict resolution through real-life human experience. www.theforgivenessproject.com

Author's Bio

Judith Toy was ordained by Zen Master and mindfulness author, Thich Nhat Hanh, as a core member of his order in 1997. She and her husband, Philip Toy, also ordained, have founded three communities of practice, and now lead days of mindfulness, workshops and retreats in the US and abroad. Judith Toy is a poet, writer and editor of non-fiction. An excerpt from this book appeared in Best Buddhist Writing 2006, published by Shambhala. She has received numerous grants and awards in literature and the arts; she has written and produced two plays, created a graduate workshop on writing for teachers, taught children from kindergarten through graduate school, and worked with homeless teens and prisoners. She lives with her husband, Philip Toy, and their two cairn terriers in Black Mountain, North Carolina.

12294741R00150

Made in the USA
Charleston, SC
25 April 2012